P9-AGF-326

Celebrating The Ministry of Healing:

Joseph Cardinal Bernardin's Reflections on Healthcare

The Catholic Health Association of the United States
St. Louis, MO, and Washington, DC

ISBN 0-87125-255-4

Printed in the United States of America.

The Catholic Health Association of the United States represents the combined strength of its members, more than 2,000 Catholic health-care sponsors, systems, facilities, and related organizations. Founded in 1915, CHA unites its members to advance selected strategic issues that are best addressed together rather than as individual organizations. It strengthens the Church's healing ministry in the United States by advocating for a just healthcare system, convening leaders to share ideas and foster collaboration, and uniting the ministry voice on critical issues.

National headquarters: 4455 Woodson Road, St. Louis, MO 63134-3797; 314-427-2500. Washington office: 1875 Eye Street, NW, Suite 1000, Washington, DC 20006-5409; 202-296-3993. Web site: www.chausa.org

Contents

Preface

I first met the then Archbishop Joseph L. Bernardin in Cincinnati in March 1981. The purpose of the meeting was to discuss the possibility of my being appointed as dean of the Athenaeum of Ohio and academic dean of Mt. St. Mary of the West Seminary in Cincinnati. Obviously, I expected that the conversation would be focused on issues related to seminary and lay ministry formation. Although those topics were addressed with much more detail than I had expected, the conversation became a wide ranging review of the challenges and opportunities facing the Church in the very early 1980s.

While the exact details of that conversation have faded, my first impressions remain vivid. First and foremost there was the gentility, warmth, and inclusivity that was later captured in the attribution "your brother Joseph." At the same time, there was the breadth and perceptivity of his intellectual and analytical skills. Permeating all of this was the depth of his faith and his profound pastoral sensitivity. It was clear that the Archbishop was not afraid to lead but his episcopal motto "as those who serve" indicated his commitment to both the content and the spirit of the Second Vatican Council.

In the years that followed, (which included serving on the Cardinal's personal staff from 1984 until his death) these first impressions not only were confirmed but deepened. His accomplishments (already many) grew, as did the crosses. Unfortunately, because of his premature death, they are now the "stuff" of which history is made.

Though every chronicler will have a different take on the highlights of his service, there are three areas which I especially remember, in addition to the grace-filled way in which he lived through the cross of false allegations and journeyed with his unwelcome but nevertheless embraced friend, death. They are his commitment to the development of a consistent ethic of life, his call to a Church divided to find the common ground that is holy ground, and his pastoral and intellectual dedication to what John Paul II has described as an essential ministry of the Church — Catholic healthcare. Just as one cannot divide an individual into distinct roles (one is simultaneously son, lover, father, friend, and worker), so, too, one cannot see these as distinct or parallel efforts. Rather, they are aspects of a brilliant mosaic whose pieces are essentially tied together and create a unique work of art that reveals the mystery that is Divine Love.

It is in this spirit that this collection of Joseph Cardinal Bernardin's writings on healthcare has been brought together. The project was initiated by the Catholic Health Association shortly after the Cardinal's death. In the last years of his life, the Cardinal had a particularly close relationship with the Association. It provided invaluable contributions to the development of some of the final parts of this collection. Mr. William Cox, then CHA executive vice president, suggested topics the Cardinal might wish to address and tirelessly assisted in the consultative process that was part of the development of many of the Cardinal's major addresses. My predecessor, Mr. Jack Curley, encouraged the Cardinal to become a member of the CHA Board of Trustees, an appointment he accepted, in part, to exemplify his commitment to the ministry the Association serves. The Cardinal was on the board at the time of his death (in fact, the Cardinal celebrated and gave the homily at the closing Eucharist of the 1995 Catholic Health Assembly in Minneapolis the day before the diagnosis of his cancer). Jack Curley, Bill Cox, and Rev. Joe Kukura (then a CHA vice president) were present in Holy Name Cathedral for the Cardinal's Mass of Christian Burial representing those in the healing ministry who had gained inspiration, strength, and direction from the Cardinal.

For me, it is a rare privilege to be serving CHA as this project is drawn to a close. All of us who are members of the Association are appreciative of the Archdiocese of Chicago allowing us to publish this collection. In a particular way, we are grateful to Rev. Alphonse Spilly, CPPS, (who served from 1983 until the Cardinal's death as special assistant to the Cardinal, and now is overseeing the publication of his writings, even as he serves as director of the Bernardin Center at the Catholic Theological Union in Chicago) for his support and assistance.

Hopefully this collection will be a living memorial not just to a great pastoral leader but to a vision of healthcare as a fundamental social good for society and the healing ministry as essential to life, work, and ministry of the Church. A ministry grounded in the person of Jesus and experienced as a "sign of hope."

Rev. Michael D. Place, STD
President and Chief Executive Officer
The Catholic Health Association
of the United States

CHAPTER 1

Ethical Dimensions of Healthcare Administration

MacEachern Lecture, American College of Hospital Administrators, Chicago, March 4, 1983

Ladies and gentlemen, thank you for your very kind welcome. I am delighted to be with you today, to share in your meeting and to offer my own reflections. And I appreciate Dr. Wesbury's invitation to deliver the 1983 Malcolm T. MacEachern Memorial Lecture.

I am particularly pleased to be with you because of the many perspectives that we share in common. I realize that to the superficial viewer our roles and responsibilities might appear to be quite different. It strikes me, on the contrary, that they are quite similar.

In fact, there is a sense in which it could be said that you and I belong to a very select fraternity, given the kind of leadership we try to offer. We are not the only members of this fraternity, of course. School principals are members. Camp directors, perhaps. Maybe even cowboys, as they try to lead herds of wild buffalo!

But you and I are similar in another, much more fundamental respect. For we both have as our core vocation the task of providing caring and careful service to our brothers and sisters in the human family.

I

I say that our service must be caring. For there is something really offensive about service, be it healthcare or religious ministry, that is not motivated by love. And conversely, when the love of the human family assumes its proper central role, then both religion and healthcare tend to reveal their kindred spirits.

It is no accident that the hospital as an institution in western society emerged as an act of religious service. It is no accident that the vocation of nursing had such an intimate connection to the charitable love of women religious for the poor, the suffering and the outcast, that to this day, in many parts of the world, nurses are called sisters. It is no accident that religious communities continue to sponsor hospitals, nursing homes, care facilities for the handicapped. Here in the Archdiocese of Chicago, for example, there are more than 20 hospitals that claim affiliation with the Roman Catholic Church, and many, many more that are rooted in the religious values of love and concern as articulated by other communities.

I do not mean to suggest that hospitals and healthcare must, in fact, be rooted in religious organizations. That is evidently not the case. But I think that it is true that the values pursued in healthcare are intrinsically related to the ethical values about the meaning of human life that are typically proclaimed by religious communities. And so I wish to speak to you about those values that I find in my faith commitment, and that you, I believe, must find some place for, if your service to the sick is to bear fruit.

> *We are called to care for one another, to support one another, walk with one another, heal one another, to help one another live, and indeed, when the time comes, to share with one another in death.*

I am speaking first and foremost of a singleminded commitment to the dignity and worth of human persons.

The times in which we live are strange and contradictory times. In some ways, human persons are more fully appreciated now than in the past; the value of human life is more cherished. Clearly we put more time and energy and money into the development of human life. We are more concerned about the cultivation of physical fitness. We are more sensitive to issues of life expectancy. We are more knowledgeable about the intricacies of good nutrition.

But for all that, our times also exhibit a frightening coldness about matters of human dignity. Too often we proclaim the beauty of the human spirit only when it is encased in the beauty of a well-formed human body. Too often we celebrate the wonder of the human being only when it comes accompanied by the wonder of a bright and articulate intellect. Too often we appreciate the value of the human person only because we perceive there the value of human productivity.

Is it because persons are useful to us that we celebrate them as good in themselves? I am sure that none of you would espouse that philosophy expressed so baldly. And yet, isn't it true that much in our contemporary culture encourages that perspective? It is talent, intellect, physical beauty, usefulness that so often serve as the grounds for human dignity.

That is not the view that religion proclaims. And it is not the view in which healthcare finds its source. Rather, our common roots lie deep in the soil of intrinsic human dignity. We are a human family, we are called to care for one another, to support one another, walk with one another, heal one another, to help one another live, and indeed, when the time comes, to share with one another in death.

I have no doubt that the implementation of this vision is fraught with difficulty. I will speak of some of these problems in a few moments. But let it be said that the energizing vision of healthcare must be this commitment to the dignity of human persons before and apart from questions of productivity. Pope John Paul II passionately proclaimed this vision when he was in the United States in 1979. On the Mall in Washington, DC, he declared: "All human beings ought to value every person for his or her uniqueness as a creature of God.... This explains our efforts to defend human life against every influence or action that threatens or weakens it, as well as our endeavors to make every life more human in all its aspects."*

This same vision is the sure consequence of the religious roots from which healthcare has grown. We must remain true to those roots. The emergency room must not take note of color. The delivery room must not administer IQ tests. The intensive care unit must not sponsor beauty contests. And the hospital must not become the implementor of a strategy of societal triage where the fittest always come first.

No, the hospital must be a place where all persons are appreciated in their dignity and loved and served for their value.

II

I am well aware of the complexity of the task that I describe. Indeed, I am conscious that in some ways it is impossible. The philosopher Leibniz said that "all things are possible, but not all things are compossible." We are finite beings, you and I, and we live in a finite world. To spend our resources here is to make them unavailable there. To care for this person can indeed sometimes result in being unable to care for that one. To commit our financial resources to one project inevitably implies the rejection or the postponement of another project.

The ethical vision that comes from the religious traditions and that is proclaimed, I may add, within the Catholic community does not deny this fact. Quite the contrary, it acknowledges it and deals with it directly.

St. Thomas Aquinas, more than 700 years ago, proclaimed that the central virtue of the ethical person is prudence. Good judgment, the skill of incarnating appropriate ideals in the flesh of concrete, complex, and contingent human variables: that is what he saw as necessary. And it is just as necessary in our time. So for you, as for me, the challenge of car-

* "Celebrate Life," Homily of Pope John Paul II on the Capitol Mall, Washington, DC, October 7, 1979, *The Pope Speaks*, vol 24, no. 4, 1979, p. 373.

ing service demands the high skill of good judgment.

And that is why I said at the beginning that our service must be both caring and careful. It must be competent and wise. You cannot do all things for all persons. You cannot provide all services to all members of the human family. The question you daily encounter, therefore, is how to serve people best. I want you to know that I appreciate the pain of the struggle that is involved in those concrete judgments. You daily find yourselves having to balance a variety of values, seeking to respond to the competing claims of different populations and different perspectives. You must often perceive yourself as the great compromiser, the politician par excellence. You are, in the ancient language, seeking to be the prudent man or woman in your highly complex situation.

But to affirm this complexity is not to deny what I said earlier. Human persons are not just variables to be manipulated in the complex casuistry of the hospital setting. Rather they are the one stable element in terms of which all other judgments are made. The dignity and value of human persons is a basic value, not to be traded against some other values, not to be entered in some subtle calculus that seeks the greatest good for the greatest number.

No, in this finite and ambiguous world, it is not always possible for us to do all good things. But it is possible for us, in the great words of the Hippocratic Oath, to "do no harm." We are challenged in our caring and careful service never to attack the fundamental value of the dignity of the human person. If we cannot always treat all of our clients with our most ambitious and imaginative resources, still we are always able to treat them, one and all, with fundamental respect.

That, for example, is the import of the wise, ancient ethical tool that distinguishes ordinary and extraordinary means of healthcare. You are well aware that those terms themselves can cause confusion, since they are used differently by ethicists and by healthcare professionals. But the key notion of the distinction is clear: that not all acts which are *possible* are *obligatory*.

Not all interventions that are conceivable are desirable. But some are. Those actions towards human persons that represent fundamental respect for their living dignity: those are not only possible, they are obligatory. For it is never an act of caring and careful service to attack human persons, to insult them, to treat them with disrespect. We must respect, cherish, and protect all human life, born and unborn, from conception until death.

It may, and indeed sometimes is, an act of caring and careful service to walk quietly with human persons toward the conclusion of their lives. The healthcare profession is, after all, in a strange position. It seeks to do a task in which it somehow always fails. For it seeks to maintain life, and yet we will all die. You have no doubt given this anomaly much thought through the years. And you have come to see that it is not your task simply to protect survival. It is your task to care for human persons, to serve the quality of life, as it is sometimes called. As long as that quality is seen as encompassing the fundamental dignity of persons, as long as it is not allowed to degenerate into some quantitative calculation of a person's utility to or for society, that insight is utterly correct. Caring and careful service involves constant respect for persons, unquestioning commitment to do no harm, and wise and prudent efforts to maximize the quality of living for all one's clients.

III

I must add some words about the particular challenges which face you as hospital administrators. I am not an expert in your field. But I am aware of some of the struggles that preoccupy you. And I would like to acknowledge them, in the process of acknowledging your important work. I facetiously commented at the beginning that your job was like that of the cowboy, herding wild buffalo. Hyperbole, no doubt. But I know that the administrator of a hospital is faced with a task not much less difficult in coordinating the efforts of so many different healthcare professionals.

The dignity and value of human persons is a basic value, not to be traded against some other values, not to be entered in some subtle calculus that seeks the greatest good for the greatest number.

The language of the "healthcare team" is used easily. The reality is created with far more difficulty. You work so hard to coordinate the efforts of physicians, nurses, dieticians, therapists of different kinds, experts in the various biological and chemical sciences. Each of these individuals has a differing perspective. Orchestrating their common commitment into an organized service is, no doubt, one of your most difficult tasks. At times, prudence must seem utterly insufficient. I'm sure there are days you wish you could have omniscience and omnipotence as well. But you are virtuous men and women in your efforts to do that coordination, living out the ideals of religious ethics in that task.

I know, too, that you struggle daily with the challenge of cost containment in hospital administration. To discuss matters of this concreteness is not to trivialize the dignity of human persons. Quite the contrary, it is to acknowledge that caring service must also be careful, that respect for persons must express itself in concrete action. What a challenge it must be for you to balance the increasing sophistication of technology and science with the possible in your setting, recognizing that in some ways *improved* healthcare competes with *accessible* healthcare. Much more is possible if there is no need to limit costs. But then it can happen that healthcare becomes the prerogative of the rich. And that, you know, does attack human dignity. And so you seek to contain costs without unduly sacrificing quality. I have no answers in your struggle to do that. It is prudence, the skill of good judgment, that provides those answers. And only you, living in the very midst of the struggles, dialoguing with your brothers and sisters in the profession, only you can have that prudence.

The techniques and strategies of business are most helpful, but healthcare is not and must never become a business. To profit from the struggles of the human spirit is, I dare say, equally obscene.

To talk of cost containment is to suggest a third area which must be an abiding concern for you. That is the allocation of limited resources. Caring and careful service, as I have said, involves the acknowledgement that we live in a finite world, that all things are not compossible. On what basis does a hospital decide the direction for its future expansion? On what grounds does a healthcare facility commit itself to development in one way or another? The allocation of our monetary resources must be done on the criteria of service to human dignity and of respect for human persons.

This is not to deny, of course, the relevance of economic considerations. The prudent style I have been suggesting makes clear that all factors are relevant. But it does mean that economics alone must never be allowed to shape the direction of the healthcare profession. Like yourselves, I must daily struggle with questions of cost containment and resource allocation. But if my religious ministry were ever allowed to become a business, if that ministry were ever allowed to lose its roots in caring and careful service, if it were to establish its fundamental identity in the profit motive, then something very contradictory and, indeed, obscene, would have happened. I dare to say that the same thing is true in your case. The techniques and strategies of business are most helpful, but healthcare is not and must never become a business. To profit from the struggles of the human spirit is, I dare say, equally obscene.

And so you struggle with the issues of resource allocation. You struggle, I know, with competing claims of primary, secondary, and tertiary healthcare. You wonder whether more service could not be provided to the human family by an emphasis upon preventive care rather than by a focus upon crisis intervention. You do this, aware of your own limitations. You do this, painfully conscious of the commitments made already, the facilities that you have, the skills that are present. And you seek to bring prudence to bear in these situations.

And you do all of this, I must add finally, in a setting where healthcare is becoming competitive. Is it the truth that we have overdeveloped this profession? Provided too many facilities of certain kinds? Must we find ourselves in the tragic setting of too much care for some and not enough for others? I do not know the answer to these questions, either. I know that you struggle with them daily.

I urge you to maintain the struggle, to continue to ask the questions, to honestly admit the ambiguities, the uncertainties, and indeed, the embarrassing errors, and to seek to build a future where healthcare is increasingly caring and careful.

IV

You are doing that already. In some sense, perhaps all of my reflections are no more than an expression of what you already think. I celebrate you for your dedicated and skillful work. It is the Christian vision, whose spokesman I am, that God made us and loves us as we are, that in his creation of us and our world, he empowered us to care for one another, to nourish one another, to heal one another, and in all our daily needs to love one another. From the perspective of this present world, there is perhaps no other service that so fully expresses this Christian and religious vision of human family as does the healthcare profession. You have a proud and beautiful vocation. I applaud you for it. And I offer you my prayerful and active support as you seek to express your service more and more effectively.

The Scriptures tell us that the men and women who comprised the early Christian community were utterly captivated by the vision they had received from Jesus. In their appropriation of that vision, they found themselves challenged to a particular style of living. That lifestyle was noticed by those around them. So we are told that the bystanders could honestly say, "See how those Christians love one another."

That same vision of life is the hallmark of the healthcare profession. Agents of health service are energized by that same vision, whether they find it in Christian faith or in some other fundamentally religious instinct. For them, for you, that vision likewise challenges to a particular style of life. And that lifestyle, too, is evident to those who stand nearby.

When it comes to healthcare service, I am a bystander. But I want you to know that this bystander can also say to you, "See how these healthcare professionals love one another. See how caring and careful they are, in their efforts to serve the human family. See how wondrous is their task. See how dedicated is their service. See how skillful is their effort."

I do see. And I admire. And I assure them—assure you—of my respect, my affection, and my prayers.

CHAPTER 2

Medicine and Religion: Toward Healing and Peace

University of Illinois Medical School,
Chicago, June 27, 1984

I am delighted to be with you today. I thank Dr. Hyman Muslin for the gracious invitation. And I thank all of you for your participation.

The topic suggested to me, one which I gladly accepted, is: How we can work together for the healing of the human person. It is an extremely challenging subject. It admits a number of possible approaches. Perhaps it would be helpful if I share with you the kind of concern which generated its formulation.

I would like to quote from Dr. Muslin's letter to me: "I now wish to tell you," he said, "as I indicated in my original invitation, why I thought it would be important for us to have you come to talk to the physicians, medical students, and nurses. We are distressed in medicine about our difficulties and our failures in being of service in the development of man. Specifically, we see eruptions of hatred and violence on all levels of the local, national, and international scene, and do not see that *our* teachings and ministrations have had sufficient impact on the capacity of man to advance in his empathy toward his fellowman and thus be able to experience other people's distresses. This developmental accomplishment, in our view, would be of greater service towards the acquisition of operational restraints against hatred and violence. Our wish to have man develop an operational humanism is, of course, shared by you as we know, and our failures are the failures of us all. We would like, if at all possible, for you to include in your remarks to us, your views on our mutual dilemma, what direction we might be taking, or what views we might entertain that would sustain us in our mission?"

As you are well aware, Dr. Muslin's questions are critically important. They are, in fact, vital; that is to say, central to our lives together. For when we dwell on the issues he raises, a core pattern emerges. The many questions begin to center on two challenges: How can we live in peace? How can we contribute to a peaceful climate in this world?

There seems to be a certain brokenness or woundedness within us that keeps us from living peacefully. If we could engage in a healing process, it would undoubtedly be better.

Although we can state the challenges simply—how to live in peace, how to contribute to peace, how to contribute toward the healing of people to bring about peace—the questions are not so simply solved. With no pretensions of claiming a complete response, I would like to offer some ideas for reflection and dialogue. I hope that these ideas—indications, as it were, of how we might approach the theme—will contribute to the wider dialogue in which we must be engaged.

Before I begin, I want to make a disclaimer and I want to clarify the intent of my comments.

The disclaimer is simply this. I am *not* an academician. In fact, you should know that the university is not my regular terrain of activity. I value theory, follow it as much as I am able; perhaps I have even been able to make modest contributions to its advancement. Overall, however, I am not a theoretician of peace and healing. I am, first and foremost, a pastor, and, therefore, engaged in the *practice* of making peace and promoting healing. It is as a pastor-practitioner that I wish to speak with you.

In other words, what I want to offer you is not a theory. Much more simply, I want to share with you how I work for the kind of healing that brings about peace. As I offer you these reflections on "my practice," I think that certain points of convergence will emerge between your work in medicine and mine as a representative of the Church. At that point, we can, through our dialogue, discover ways of deeper collaboration rooted in a common purpose.

By way of an overview of my remarks, let me note that I will share four areas of activity on different levels of life: My concern for global peace, my initiatives on behalf of a consistent ethic of life, my service to Chicago, and, finally, my own inner life and personal quest for healing and peace. So let me begin these remarks, which I would categorize as "reflective sharings."

World Peace Initiatives

I am deeply concerned, as no doubt you are also, about the survival of the human race, the survival of our planet. Our survival is threatened by the ever-increasing arsenal of nuclear weapons, by an arms race which seems to be out of control. Together with the other Catholic bishops in the United States, I was involved in the development and dissemination of a pastoral letter entitled, *The Challenge of Peace: God's Promise and Our Response*. Because we represent a voice for the Roman Catholic Church in our nation, because we passionately emphasized the urgency of coming to terms with the questions posed by the nuclear age, because we strongly encouraged both our own Catholic people and other citizens to see the questions of war and peace as crucial moral issues—because of all this, there has been a great deal of media coverage and publicity. Although many people have been involved, as chairman of the committee that drafted the letter, I have personally received quite a bit of attention. In itself, that attention and recognition are, of course, quite secondary when dealing with issues of survival. But from that experience, I have developed two insights: the first is in regard to the way I must look at the world; the second, the role I must play.

I am deeply concerned about the survival of the human race, the survival of our planet. Our survival is threatened by the ever-increasing arsenal of nuclear weapons, by an arms race which seems to be out of control.

I have come to learn that I must look at the world and its problems of survival and achieving peace in a particular way. By instinct, I would have tended to look at particular problems as single and specific concerns. However, through study, prayer, and analysis, I have come to appreciate the perspective of the "total system." I may not be able to grasp all the parts of our world's woundedness and brokenness that lead us to the brink of international disaster. But I have come to appreciate how the parts are interconnected and need to be addressed in a more comprehensive fashion. There are links, for example, between the build-up of arms and the continued poverty of large parts of the world. There are links between diminished or reduced understandings of the true dignity of the human person, reduced perhaps to a functional component of the state, and the propensity to international violence. These are just two examples of the linkage that exists among the various issues confronting us in our contemporary society. If I want to grasp these issues more fully, I must see them as part of a larger picture, as part of a totality.

A second personal insight which came to me through my work on the peace pastoral was a deeper understanding of the role I am to play. I came to understand that my role, quite simply, is to be a voice. I am called, both by my position and my own inner sense, to be a voice—someone who articulates the concern. In our letter on the challenge of peace, for example, we did not offer detailed technical or political strategies. That would be beyond our competence. Our task, rather, was to voice the concern; to provide a moral vision, a framework within which people could make their own moral analysis of the issues. In an era of specialization, such as our own, it is perhaps unusual for one not to offer the solution to particular questions, but simply to raise the questions themselves and to do so in a way that makes other people take notice. I have come to understand my role in the healing and peacemaking process in this way. I am a voice.

Initiatives Concerning a Consistent Ethic of Life

In recent months, I have engaged in a dialogue—a debate, really—which has involved not only the Catholic community but the broader community as well. The specific theme of this debate is the need to promote what I have called a "consistent ethic of life."

At Fordham University last December and at St. Louis University this spring, I spoke of the various life issues confronting our society as constituting a "seamless garment." By that I mean that there is a linkage among such issues as abortion, war, hunger, human rights, euthanasia, and capital punishment; they belong in a common discussion, although the specific issues themselves are not identical and each requires its own moral analysis.

Reaction to the Fordham presentation, mainly within the Catholic Church but also others, was rapid and strong. Some of the responses stated that abortion and capital punishment are not identical issues. The principle which protects innocent life distinguishes the unborn child from the convicted murderer. Other letters stressed that, while nuclear war is a threat to life, abortion involves the actual taking of life, here and now. I accept both of these distinctions, of course, but I also find compelling the need to relate the cases while keeping them in distinct categories. Abortion, the direct taking of unborn life, is constantly increasing in our society. Those concerned about it, I believe, will find their case enhanced by taking note of the rapidly expanding use of capital punishment. In a similar way, those who are particularly concerned about these executions, even if the accused has taken another life, should recognize the elementary truth that a society which is indifferent to the life of an innocent, unborn child will not be easily stirred to concern for a convicted criminal. Aside from the moral considerations, there is, I maintain, a political and psychological linkage among

Working for the healing of the human person requires an integrated and unified vision of the underlying values which are at stake.

the life issues—from war to welfare concerns—which we ignore at our own peril: a comprehensive vision of life seeks to expand the moral horizon of society, not partition it into airtight categories.

I put it this way in my recent St. Louis lecture: "Each of the issues I have identified today—abortion, war, hunger and human rights, euthanasia, and capital punishment—is treated as a separate, self-contained topic in our public life. Each is distinct, but an ad hoc approach to each one fails to illustrate how our choices in one area can affect our decisions in other areas. There must be a public attitude of respect for all of life, if public actions are to respect it in concrete cases."

Our topic today is: working together toward the healing of the human person. From my reflections concerning a consistent ethic of life and my effort to get people to consider seriously the linkage among the many life issues, I have learned that working for the healing of the human person requires an integrated and unified vision of the underlying values which are at stake. Unless our understanding of the human person is rooted in a set of coherent, unified values, our attempts to promote healing and growth will accomplish little, given the diversity and complexity of the many issues which clamor for our attention today. We who are committed to serving human persons, our brothers and sisters, in a wholistic fashion, will become fragmented and broken in our attempts to be of service.

As with the question of peace issues, so too with the consistent ethic of life, I have come to see a specific task for myself. With regard to peace issues, as I noted earlier, I see my role as that of being a "voice." From my concern and involvement in efforts to promote a consistent ethic of life by introducing it into our national dialogue, I have come to see my task as that of a connecting memory for my people. I feel called to help people remember the foundations of their values and to remember in such a way that they can connect the issues and deal with them creatively and effectively. The task of being a connecting memory for people is particularly important for me. For in providing this "service," I am able to help promote the healing of the human person, a task which is central to my ministry as a priest and bishop.

Service to Chicago

Another way in which I have invested myself in the ministry of healing is through my commitment to the people of Chicagoland, that is, the people of both the city and the metropolitan area. Chicago is an amazing mosaic of people who are different in color, in language, in culture—in a sense, different in everything except a common humanity and, I believe, a common potential for greatness and for mutual enrichment.

At the same time, it is quite evident that in many ways we are a divided city. We are divided racially, ethnically, socially, and economically. We are divided perhaps in as many ways as we are different. The divisions isolate us from each other and lead us to a climate which favors suspicion rather than trust, despair rather than hope, monotony rather than creativity, a climate which sometimes leads even to violence.

As the Roman Catholic Archbishop of Chicago, as a person who believes that we are destined to be together and find new life and wholeness through our different gifts, I seek various ways to promote the unity of Chicago. This is no easy task. The woundedness and brokenness of the city have developed over a long period of time. For example, it was restrictive covenants in housing, developed in the early part of this century, that led to the stinging effects of racial segregation which we feel so sharply today. But I try not to let the magnitude of the difficulties discourage me or my collaborators. We are seeking something very simple. As a Church which is committed to being a healing agent in the community of Chicago, we seek to develop patterns of compassion which can be expressed in concrete ways.

The proclamation of an ideal such as practical, concrete compassion—literally the specific ability to suffer with others and to celebrate with them—can be empty rhetoric. So often it is easy to convince oneself that *saying* something is the equivalent of *doing* something. So it has been the intent and the effort of the Church in Chicago to concretize in specific actions the compassion with which we hope to embrace all people. This has happened through our outreach to the entire community, especially through education, healthcare, and social services. We have tried to be as inclusive as possible. All of this is an attempt to specify in action the kind of compassion and tolerance we seek to call forth from the people of Chicago.

> *We are divided racially, ethnically, socially, and economically.*

As I reflect on my task in this ministry of extending concrete compassion to the people in our city, I see myself primarily as an educator. I take that word "educator" in its Latin root sense as "one who draws out." A teacher is not merely one who lectures or talks about issues. A teacher can teach by doing, by indicating, by prodding, by accompanying those taught in certain directions. I see myself as a person who is learning both the ways of inclusion and compassion as I come to understand and serve the city better; I see myself as someone who is encouraging others to make connections.

Through this sort of educational process, I hope that I am contributing in my own way to the healing of the divisions and woundedness that mar Chicago and cut short the greatness that is our possibility.

My Inner Life and Personal Quest for Healing and Peace

In these reflective sharings concerning my approach to healing and internal peace, I have spoken of my involvement in working for world peace, in working for a national consensus regarding the values which are at the heart of the life issues, and in working for a compassion and connection among the many diverse elements of the Chicago experience. I would like now to share still another level and dimension of my involvement in working for healing and for peace. This has to do with myself.

The questions of peace and healing are not simply issues "out there" on an international, national, or city scale. They are also issues that affect me in a deep and personal way. They are as much a part of me as they are of the world within which I live.

About seven years ago, I came to understand that the pace of my life and the direction of my activity were unfocused, uncentered in a significant way. I am not talking simply about the organization of time and energy for efficient work. The issues were really issues of the spirit, that is, I found myself unpeaceful and in need of healing. I came to understand, through the assistance of people who had already passed through this kind of personal journey toward healing, wholeness, and peace, that I, too, had to make changes.

It would be difficult for me to elaborate this set of changes in this context. So many elements—in fact, the core elements—are tied to my personal faith and belief system. Let me say this much, however. I found that the way to healing, peace, and wholeness meant that I had to have a centered life. I needed a renewal of prayer in my life.

Mention of prayer may evoke an image of "saying" prayers, of reciting formulas, of incantations of one sort or another. I mean something quite different. When I speak of the renewal of prayer in my life, I am speaking of reconnecting myself with the larger mystery of life and of my common existence with other people. This certainly involves a certain kind of discipline in the use of time; it requires, too, some exercise of centering. But the essential ingredient is a contemplative stance toward life. An attitude of openness that will be ready to receive what the larger mystery we call God has to offer me—by way of insight, perspectives, feelings, sense of values, inspiration, and so forth.

This has been a remarkably rich, even if not always easy, path toward healing, wholeness, and a peaceful way of life. I have found myself called to be a contemplator in the widest and the narrowest sense of that word; one who gazes and looks beyond the surface, or, rather, one who allows the depth dimension of life to surface. I am not an expert in this. I am no guru. I am a learner, and I dialogue in a process we call spiritual direction about my prayer. The point I wish to make is simply this. The approach to healing, wholeness, and peace on the many levels of life that we have considered includes, in my experience, the decisive and crucial level of one's own personal self.

Conclusion

Dr. Muslin in his invitation spoke of the possibility of cooperation. I think that he meant the cooperation, collaboration, and the mutual reenforcement that might take place between those in the Church who are concerned with healing and those in medicine who are also concerned and dedicated to the healing process. The overall view is one that goes much deeper than the physical, material level. While not ignoring that level, the question is how we might come to live a more peaceful life, and how a healing process might be promoted to that end.

> ***My role was that of an educator, calling people to understand the need for compassion.***

What I have attempted to do is to offer you some reflective sharings of my own approach to healing and the search for a more peaceful life. I spoke of these in terms of the various levels of my involvement: the questions of international peace, the issues of life that face our nation, the move toward compassion and pluralism in our city, and, finally, my personal quest for healing and wholeness through a contemplative-prayerful attitude in life.

Are my own strivings so idiosyncratic as to preclude the possibility of others sharing them? I think not. I believe that if the question is a shared vision and a shared strategy in working for the healing—the integral healing—of the human person, then we can share many elements together and reenforce our efforts.

When I spoke of my efforts for the cause of world peace, I spoke of my own insight into the need to deal with the larger systems and my own task in the process as that of being a voice that raises the issues and questions. Are these also not possible for people in the healing professions? That you would more clearly attend to the larger picture, the larger systems that give meaning to life, and voice your concern through whatever forum is available—is that not a real, viable, and effective kind of option?

When I spoke of my approach to life issues in the United States, I spoke of the linkage of the issues, how they are rooted in fundamental values which I consider it my task to recall and connect. Is this not also the task of people involved in medicine? Are you not also called to make the strenuous effort to understand the basic values that underlie so many disparate issues of human hurting, woundedness, and violence? Rather than moving in an ad hoc way on each of these issues, would it not be better to probe reflectively, philosophically, perhaps even religiously, into the underlying values that illuminate, give meaning to, and link together a broad spectrum of questions?

When I talked about my service to the city of Chicago, I spoke of a task of healing that involves bringing together many disparate parts, of creating a climate of tolerance, compassion, and inclusivity. I felt that my role was that of an educator, calling people to understand the need for compassion and what it means, in the concrete, to be compassionate. Is this not also a concern for the medical profession? For example, what are the implications of compassion in the delivery of healthcare services, in the distribution of skills and energy? The balancing of market values with human compassion in such a way that the public sees and recognizes in you a genuine commitment to contribute to the healing of human persons—that must be your goal and, if you realize it, it will make a great difference in you personally and in this community. Your success in this regard will truly have healing effects which will go far beyond yourselves.

Lastly, I spoke of my own journey and struggles toward wholeness, of being in touch with the larger mystery of life through a contemplative stance. Is this not the necessary path for all healers, that they themselves be in touch with their own need for healing, for making peace in their own hearts? From this, they can draw on reserves of experience and humanity which will serve their patients well.

I hope, through these reflections, that I have been able to communicate several things.

First, I hope you realize how important I find the topic that has been raised by this conference.

Second, I hope you appreciate how deeply I feel about your contribution to the healing of the human person and, indeed, the healing of human society.

Third, I hope you understand that the way to develop clearer insight into these deep and complex matters is not through abstract deductions but through a process of shared experience and wisdom, such as we are engaged in at this moment.

Finally, I hope and I pray that you will continue this quest on many different levels, that your involvements will not be limited to the treatment of specific diseases but that you will also search out the roots of our woundedness and apply the healing remedies there.

CHAPTER 3

A Vision of the Human Person and Ethical Choices

Illinois Hospital Association,
Chicago, November 8, 1984

I wish to thank Kenneth Robbins and the Illinois Hospital Association Board of Trustees for the opportunity to address you this afternoon. To some degree, I have an outsider's view of healthcare facilities, but it is a rather privileged one. The Archdiocese of Chicago is blessed with 24 Catholic hospitals and nearly 20 Catholic nursing and retirement homes. In addition, we provide pastoral care services at many other hospitals.

There is a generally accepted consensus that persons under medical care are not simply two-legged animals who can be successfully treated by the canons of veterinary medicine. Human medicine cares for human persons, and even our sophisticated contemporary medicine does not fully understand the human person. Human persons are walking enigmas, talking mysteries, autonomous individuals who can never be reduced to the fictional 98 cents worth of chemicals we might recover at an autopsy. Today we are becoming more aware of how the condition of the whole person affects the healing process.

This broad notion of healing suggests that physicians and nurses do not have a monopoly as agents of healing. Persons engaged in pastoral care are healers, too, as are caregivers from among family and friends. Needless to say, this is not to minimize the marvelous success of our healing institutions or to overlook the dramatic advances they have made by comparison with hospitals at the turn of the century.

Nevertheless hospitals today face another set of challenges, including the rapid development and cost escalation of technology, decreased governmental aid for patients who are poor, and overall cost containment. These, in turn, raise a variety of ethical issues for healthcare providers.

You are addressing many ethical issues at this annual meeting. What I propose to do this afternoon is reflect on a vision of the human person which underlies the ethical choices we make. While I will speak from my perspective as a Roman Catholic bishop, most of what I will say will transcend denominational beliefs. My purpose is to sketch out a broad outline of medical humanism, which will help put such issues as proper use of technology and care for the poor in appropriate perspective.

Published originally in *Health Progress*, April 1985.

Ethical Questions Raised in Medicine

Let me begin by briefly considering the kinds of ethical questions raised by the progress of medical science today. Clearly not all of our scientific achievements are automatically self-justifying. The fact that we *can* explode a hydrogen bomb, does not mean we are justified in doing so. By the same token, the fact that we *can* develop a test-tube human baby does not necessarily mean that we are justified in doing that.

Do different versions of humanism provide different norms and set different limits upon our self-manipulation? I think they do, and we should carefully examine and articulate the kind of humanism we are following. For example, how far should individual persons be subordinated to an abstract goal of human progress or the future common good?

Our own present skill in caring for handicapped babies and children presents such a question. Does humanism encourage use of public resources for such neonatal intensive care, or does it rather encourage us to quietly dispose of such individuals for the sake of the common good? Does humanism support personal procreative parenthood, or does it suggest laboratory reproduction in the hope of guaranteeing stronger, healthier specimens of humanity? How do we respond to the ethical implications of the transplant of a baboon's heart into an infant? What are the implications of this action in regard to human experimentation?

The critical aspect of medical achievements is the fact that we are experimenting upon ourselves, not on animals, plants, or inorganic nature. Medical research, therefore, rightly looks to humanism for some norms and guidance in this self-experimentation.

Humanism

All physicians as well as all patients are humanists in their own individual ways. All of us have our own conceptualizations of human dignity and our own definition of "being human..." Possibly we have specific convictions about how our human race originated, or if and how the world will end. These convictions may well rest on scientific data, but each of us reflects upon that data and—with the help of intuition, reasoning, the accumulated wisdom of the ages, and, often enough, religious faith—we reach our personal convictions and establish our own personal brand of humanism.

If our humanism includes a personal God as Creator and Lord of the universe, we may designate it a religious humanism. Nonreligious versions of humanism avoid the concept of God and may seem at first glance to give added dignity and autonomy to human persons because there is no notion of submission or subservience to a Creator. But it should be noted immediately that these nonreligious versions of humanism sometimes tend to exalt humanity even at the expense of individual persons. They do not always defend the full personal dignity of individuals.

I do not think all versions of nonreligious humanism appearing in the course of history would answer questions about individual persons and the common good of humanity in the same way. I suggest that we can distinguish two major kinds of humanism according to the emphasis they place on either pragmatic concerns or on the inherent value of the person. I will call them *pragmatic* humanism and *personalist* humanism. Both kinds are called humanism because both recognize human potential; both seek to foster human progress and civilization. But they are distinguished in that pragmatic humanism gives priority to some form of human progress, and personalist humanism gives priority to persons as persons.

The critical aspect of medical achievements is the fact that we are experimenting upon ourselves, not on animals.

1. Pragmatic Humanism

Pragmatic humanism tends to reckon human dignity in terms of human functioning or *praxis*. One is human in action terms: doing, producing, thinking, achieving. This key consideration determines who is most fully human, although human dignity may be accorded to others as well. In this case these others do not actually enjoy full human dignity *per se*. Rather it is the community that finds it appropriate to treat such individuals with human dignity. Hence in this view, fetuses and newborn babies, the comatose, the insane, and the hopelessly senile may not actually enjoy full human dignity even though society may have generally attributed it to them.

Because of this social attribution of human dignity even to nonproductive or useless persons, pragmatic humanism can accept most of the social and institutional policies which presently protect these individuals. But it must be remembered that this situation is subject to social change. In this theory, which emphasizes the pragmatic dignity or value of persons, those whose lives are nonproductive, useless, or without social meaning have only an extrinsically attributed dignity. Such dignity is clearly subject to cost-benefit analysis and the manipulation of social engineers in a politically sophisticated society.

Implicit in pragmatic humanism is the fact that society may diminish the value and dignity of nonproductive persons for the sake of the common welfare because that is the very reason such value and dignity was attributed in the first place. This kind of humanism goes hand in hand with the social contract theory of human rights since it sees rights as under the control of those who contract to form society. If the social consensus favors narrowing the extent of those enjoying full human dignity and rights it does so, more or less, in the tradition of "might makes right."

Personalist humanism recognizes a moral equality of all living human persons, regardless of their age, race, color, or creed.

Our American tradition does not espouse the extreme kind of pragmatic humanism just described, at least not in general practice. Yet there is a logic and a consistency in this view which attracts some serious thinkers today. Those who feel that political authority can act independently of a higher moral law might permit political authorities to apply this pragmatic humanism in lessening welfare and public health budgets. Such pragmatic policymakers might recommend compulsory amniocentesis of all pregnant women and consequent compulsory abortion of all defective fetuses. They might support government funding of artificial human breeding and compulsory euthanasia for the senile and for severely defective infants.

The reason for presenting this sketch of pragmatic humanism is not to sound a doomsday warning. I am personally hopeful that as new medical research offers new opportunities for a callous and pragmatic type of humanism, we will recommit ourselves to the personalist humanism which is central to modern democracy and our own American traditions.

2. Personalist Humanism

Personalist humanism believes in the inherent value and dignity of every living human person even though unwanted or unvalued by others. Personalist humanism teaches that inherent rights accompany inherent dignity, specifically the rights to life and liberty found in our U.S. Declaration of Independence. Personalist humanism recognizes a *moral equality* of all living human persons, regardless of their age, intelligence, degree of social adaptability, state of health or social usefulness, race, color, or creed.

Therefore, personalist humanism rejects the killing of any innocent living persons or the sacrificing of their inherent rights by subjecting them to discrimination or to medical experimentation or manipulation without their consent. Personalist humanism in the political order is expressed by innumerable modern declarations of human rights, including that of the United Nations. It clearly opposes attacks on the rights of any individuals, whether they are political dissidents, defective infants, or senile grandparents. Personalist humanism, nonetheless, does not constitute an idolatrous worship of human life as an absolute good. It does not insist that society must use *every possible* form of technology to keep alive every suffering, comatose, or dying person. This would make the dignity of life a "taboo" principle in the tradition of magic and superstition. Personalist humanism recognizes the finite limitations of human resources and the *reasonable* limits to society's obligation to prolong human lives. But it insists on taking reasonable care of every living human person and finds an inherent contradiction in directly destroying the lives of innocent citizens. I believe that a consistent following of personalist humanism clearly forbids all forms of compulsory or involuntary euthanasia.

The philosophical foundation of personalist humanism is a conviction about human dignity which discovers that dignity as rooted in "being human" rather than "doing human things." This does not mean that human achievements and the dynamic growth of human personality are unimportant or not immensely valuable. But it does mean that one is already a person before one acts like one. It means that human equality comes from the fact of being human rather than any given threshold of human achievement. It means that no two of us are exactly equal to each other in anything, because of our individual heredity and environment, except in the initial fact of our humanness.

Implications for Medical Humanism

Most people admit that all scientific achievements do not necessarily advance the good of the human family. Technology at the service of massive war machines disgusts many of the very scientists who invented the technology. Just as steel can be used for swords or plowshares, so computers, new drugs, and new forms of surgery carry their own inner ambivalence. Many sensitive people who shuddered at the napalm deforestation of Vietnam also shudder at the advertisements in medical journals of the latest suction equipment for abortions. Even without such an emotionally charged example, one can cite the increasing depersonalization of medical practice when patients are bewildered by the process of referral to specialists, laboratories, and hospital emergency rooms. This may, of course, be the inescapable cost for greatly increased efficiency in healthcare.

The point at issue, though, is the needed value judgment which directs the use of new technology and achievement. Medical schools are increasingly striving to affirm a strong and humane element in the practice of sophisticated medicine. Advancing technology, whether in medicine or other professions, must not be permitted to threaten the moral equality of all persons.

Authentic medical humanism suggests that health professionals must direct their amazing therapeutic powers to the good of all—including the least valued and least wanted persons, symbolizing to them the love and concern which they deserve.

I realize this goal seems almost impossible in the face of rising hospital costs, increasing longevity with overflowing nursing homes, and state institutions that struggle for their very survival in budget battles.

But consider the alternative of discriminating against the nonproducers and the unwanted: an abdication of the principle of moral equality. Saving money by aborting unwanted fetuses or offering easy death to the elderly actually implies subtly that "might makes right." Those possessed of health and power are indeed mighty, but they are called by the conscience of humanism to use their gifts for the benefit of all persons.

Many in our society are attracted by the seeming efficiency of abortion and euthanasia in solving human problems. But succumbing to that attraction becomes symptomatic of another, much greater, problem: the erosion of the dignity of human personhood. As you know, the Catholic Church has maintained a constant opposition to practices like abortion and euthanasia. But we have an equal responsibility to help find better solutions to the needs of the newly born, the aging, and all persons in between.

Medical humanism today must face the challenge of cost/benefit and quality of life calculations. If the strong pressures urging such calculations are not resisted, human dignity will vary in direct ratio to a person's health or social usefulness. The unborn child and the individuals who are institutional wards of the state are clearly the test cases of our humanity and our commitment to the moral equality of all human persons. In a free society there is no substitute for dialogue about such test cases which trouble our humanist conscience. Physicians, in particular, must participate in that debate.

Let me be clear about this: You cannot do *all* things for *all* persons. You cannot provide all services to all members of the human family. The question you daily encounter, therefore, is how to serve people best. I want you to know that I appreciate the pain of the struggle that is involved in those concrete judgments. You daily find yourselves having to balance a variety of values, seeking to respond to the competing claims of different populations and different perspectives. You must often perceive yourselves as the great compromisers.

But to affirm this complexity is not to deny what I said earlier. Human persons are not just variables to be manipulated in the complex casuistry of the hospital setting. Rather they are the one stable element in light of which all other judgments are made. The dignity and value of human persons are basic values, not to be traded against some other values, not to be entered in some subtle calculus that seeks the greatest good for the greatest number.

No, in this finite and ambiguous world, it is not always possible for us to do all things. But it is possible for us, in the great words of the Hippocratic Oath, to "do no harm."

We are challenged in our caring and careful service never to attack the fundamental value of the dignity of the human person. If we cannot always treat all of our clients with our most ambitious and imaginative resources, still we are always able to treat them, one and all, with fundamental respect.

I know, too, that you struggle daily with the challenge of cost containment in hospital administration. To discuss matters of this concreteness is not to trivialize the dignity of human persons. Quite the contrary, it is to acknowledge that caring service must also be careful, that respect for persons must express itself in concrete action. What a challenge it must be for you to balance the increasing sophistication of technology and science with the possible in your setting, recognizing that in some ways *improved* healthcare competes with *accessible* healthcare. Much more is possible if there is no need to limit costs. But then it can happen that healthcare becomes the prerogative of the rich. And that, you know, does attack human dignity. And so you seek to contain costs without unduly sacrificing quality.

I have no answers in your struggle to do all this. It is prudence, the skill of good judgment, that provides the answers. And living in the very midst of the struggles, dialoguing with your brothers and sisters in the profession—only you can have that prudence. What I am suggesting is that economics alone must never be allowed to shape the direction of the healthcare profession.

Like yourselves, I must daily struggle with questions of cost containment and resource allocation. But if my religious ministry were ever allowed to become a business, if that ministry were ever allowed to lose its roots in caring and careful service, if it were to establish its fundamental identity in the profit motive, then something very contradictory and indeed, obscene, would have happened. I dare to say that the same thing is true in your case. The techniques and strategies of business are most helpful, but healthcare is not and must never become a business. To profit from the struggles of the human spirit is, I dare say, equally obscene.

As I noted at the outset, when it comes to healthcare service, I am a bystander. But I do see what you are doing. I know of your struggles. I share your concern about having to balance limited resources with needs which sometimes seem overwhelming.

In short, I admire your dedication and commitment to serving the human family. I assure you of my deepest respect, my heartfelt affection, and my prayers.

CHAPTER 4

The Consistent Ethic of Life and Healthcare Systems

Loyola University of Chicago,
May 8, 1985

We meet on an auspicious day to explore more effective ways of preserving, protecting, and fostering human life—the 40th anniversary of the end of the war in Europe which claimed millions of lives, both European and American. It was also a war in which, tragically, the word Holocaust will be forever emblazoned in history. We must never forget!

This anniversary is a day not only for remembering victory over the forces of oppression which led to this savage destruction of life but also for recommitting ourselves to preserving and nurturing all human life.

Daily we encounter news headlines which reflect the growing complexity of contemporary life, the rapid development of science and technology, the global competition for limited natural resources, and the violence which is so rampant in parts of our nation and world. The problems of contemporary humanity are enormously complex, increasingly global, and ominously threatening to human life and human society. Each of them has moral and religious dimensions because they all impact human life.

At times we may feel helpless and powerless as we confront these issues. It is crucial that we develop a method of moral analysis which will be comprehensive enough to recognize the linkages among the issues, while respecting the individual nature and uniqueness of each. During the past year and a half, I have addressed this task through the development of a "consistent ethic of life"—popularly referred to as the "seamless garment" approach to the broad spectrum of life issues.

I come before you today as a *pastor*, not a healthcare professional or theoretician, not a philosopher, not a politician, or a legal expert. As a pastor, I wish to share with you the teaching of the Catholic Church as it pertains to human life issues.

Published originally in *Linacre Quarterly*, November 1985, and in *Consistent Ethic of Life*, Sheed & Ward, Kansas City, MO, 1988.

I am very grateful to Father Baumhart for the invitation to address you on "The Consistent Ethic of Life and Healthcare Systems." I will first briefly describe the concept of a consistent ethic. Then I will explore the challenge it poses to healthcare systems both in terms of "classical" medical ethics questions and in regard to "contemporary" social justice issues.

1. The Consistent Ethic of Life

Although the consistent ethic of life needs to be finely tuned and carefully structured on the basis of values, principles, rules, and applications to specific cases, this is not my task this afternoon. I will simply highlight some of its basic components so that I can devote adequate attention to its application to healthcare systems and the issues they face today.

Catholic social teaching is based on two truths about the human person: human life is both sacred and social. Because we esteem human life as sacred, we have a duty to protect and foster it at all stages of development, from conception to death, and in all circumstances. Because we acknowledge that human life is also social, we must develop the kind of societal environment that protects and fosters its development.

Precisely because life is sacred, the taking of even one human life is a momentous event. While the presumption of traditional Catholic teaching has always been against taking human life, it has allowed the taking of human life in particular situations by way of exception—for example, in self-defense and capital punishment. In recent decades, however, the presumptions against taking human life have been strengthened and the exceptions made ever more restrictive.

Fundamental to this shift in emphasis is a more acute perception of the multiple ways in which life is threatened today. Obviously such questions as war, aggression, and capital punishment have been with us for centuries; they are not new. What is new is the *context* in which these ancient questions arise, and the way in which a new context shapes the *content* of our ethic of life.

One of the major cultural factors affecting human life today is technology. Because of nuclear weapons we now threaten life on a scale previously unimaginable—even after the horrible experience of World War II. Likewise, modern medical technology opens new opportunities for care, but it also poses potential new threats to the sanctity of life. Living, as we do, in an age of careening technological development means we face a qualitatively new range of moral problems.

The protection, defense, and nurture of human life involve the whole spectrum of life from conception to death, cutting across such issues as genetics, abortion, capital punishment, modern warfare, and the care of the terminally ill. Admittedly these are all distinct problems, enormously complex, and deserving individual treatment. No single answer and no simple response will solve them all. They cannot be collapsed into one problem, but they must be confronted as pieces of a *larger pattern.* The fact that we face new challenges in each of these areas reveals the need for a consistent ethic of life.

The precondition for sustaining a consistent ethic is a "respect life" attitude or atmosphere in society. Where human life is considered "cheap" and easily "wasted," eventually nothing is held as sacred and all lives are in jeopardy. The purpose of proposing a consistent ethic of life is to argue that success on any one of the issues threatening life requires a concern for the broader attitude in society about respect for life. Attitude is the place to root an ethic of life. Change of attitude, in turn, can lead to change of policies and practices in our society.

Besides rooting this ethic in societal attitude, I have demonstrated, in a number of recent addresses, that there is an inner relationship—a linkage—among the several issues at the more specific level of moral principle. It is not my intention to repeat these arguments today.

Nevertheless, I would like to examine briefly the relationship between "right to life" and "quality of life" issues. If one contends, as we do, that the right of every unborn child should be protected by civil law and supported by civil consensus, then our moral, political, and economic responsibilities do not stop at the moment of birth! We must defend the *right to life* of the weakest among us; we must also be supportive of the *quality of life* of the powerless among us: the old and the young, the hungry and the homeless, the undocumented immigrant and the unemployed worker, the sick, the disabled, and the dying. I contend that the viability and credibility of the "seamless garment" principle depends upon the consistency of its application.

Such a quality-of-life posture translates into specific political and economic positions—for example, on tax policy, generation of employment, welfare policy, nutrition and feeding programs, and healthcare. Consistency means we cannot have it both ways: we cannot urge a compassionate society and vigorous public and private policy to protect the rights of the unborn and then argue that compassion and significant public and private programs on behalf of the needy undermine the moral fiber of society or that they are beyond the proper scope of governmental responsibility or that of the private sector. Neither can we do the opposite!

The inner relationship among the various life issues is far more intricate than I can sketch here this afternoon. I fully acknowledge this. My intention is merely to bring that basic linkage into focus so I can apply it to the issues facing healthcare systems today.

2. The Consistent Ethic and "Classical" Medical Ethics Questions

As I noted at the outset, the consistent ethic of life poses a challenge to two kinds of problems. The first are "classical" medical ethics questions which today include revolutionary techniques from genetics to the technologies of prolonging life. How do we define the problems and what does it mean to address them from a Catholic perspective?

The essential question in the technological challenge is this: In an age when we *can* do almost anything, how do we decide what we *should* do? The even more demanding question is: in a time when we can do anything *technologically*, how do we decide *morally* what we should *not* do? My basic thesis is this: Technology must not be allowed to hold the health of human beings as a hostage.

In an address in Toronto last September, Pope John Paul II outlined three temptations of pursuing technological development:

1. Pursuing development for its own sake, as if it were an autonomous force with built-in imperatives for expansion, instead of seeing it as a resource to be placed at the service of the human family

2. Tying technological development to the logic of profit and constant economic expansion without due regard for the rights of workers or the needs of the poor and helpless

3. Linking technological development to the pursuit or maintenance of power instead of using it as an instrument of freedom.

The response to these temptations, as the Holy Father pointed out, is *not* to renounce the technological application of scientific discoveries. We need science and technology to help solve the problems of humanity. We also need to subject technological application to moral analysis.

One of the most recent and most critical ethical questions which impacts the quality of human life is that of genetics, genetic counseling, and engineering. Perhaps no other discovery in medicine has the potential so radically to change the lives of individuals and, indeed, the human race itself.

As with most scientific achievements in medicine, there are advantages and disadvantages to the utilization of this theoretical knowledge and technological know-how. Many genetic diseases can now be diagnosed early, even *in utero*, and technology is also moving toward treatment in utero. Proper use of such information can serve to prepare parents for the arrival of a special infant or can allay the fears of the expectant parents if the delivery of a healthy infant can be anticipated. The accumulation of scientific data can lead to a better understanding of the marvels of creation and to the possible manipulation of genes to prevent disease or to effect a cure before the infant sustains a permanent disability.

On the other hand, people also use available diagnostic procedures to secure information for the sex selection of their children. Some may wish to use it to eliminate "undesirables" from society. Many believe that the provision of genetic information contributes to an increase in the number of abortions.

At the other end of life's spectrum is care of the elderly. Our marvelous progress in medical knowledge and technology has made it possible to preserve the lives of newborns who would have died of natural causes not too many years ago; to save the lives of children and adults who would formerly have succumbed to contagious diseases and traumatic injuries; to prolong the lives of the elderly as they experience the debilitating effects of chronic illness and old age. At the same time, some openly advocate euthanasia, implying that we have absolute dominion over life rather than stewardship. This directly attacks the sacredness of each human life.

We need science and technology to help solve the problems of humanity. We also need to subject technological application to moral analysis.

Other new moral problems have been created by the extension of lives in intensive care units and intensive neonatal units as well as by surgical transplants and inplants, artificial insemination, and some forms of experimentation. Computers provide rapid, usually accurate, testing and treatment, but they also create problems of experimentation, confidentiality, and dehumanization. Intense debate is being waged about the extension of lives solely through extraordinary—mechanical or technological—means.

The consistent ethic of life, by taking into consideration the impact of technology on the full spectrum of life issues, provides additional insight to the new challenges which "classical" medical ethics questions face today. It enables us to define the problems in terms of their impact on human life and to clarify what it means to address them from a Catholic perspective.

3. The Consistent Ethic of Life and "Contemporary" Social Justice Issues.

The second challenge which the consistent ethic poses concerns "contemporary" social justice issues related to healthcare systems. The primary question is: How does the evangelical option for the poor shape healthcare today?

Some regard the problem as basically financial: How do we effectively allocate limited resources? A serious problem today is the fact that many persons are left without basic healthcare while large sums of money are invested in the treatment of a few by means of exceptional, expensive measures. While technology has provided the industry with many diagnostic and therapeutic tools, their inaccessibility, cost, and sophistication often prevent their wide distribution and use.

Government regulations and restrictions, cut-backs in health programs, the maldistribution of personnel to provide adequate services are but a few of the factors which contribute to the reality that many persons do not and probably will not receive the kind of basic care that nurtures life—unless we change attitudes, policies, and programs.

Public health endeavors such as home care, immunization programs, health education, and other preventive measures to improve the environment and thus prevent disease, have all served as alternate means of providing care and improving the health of the poor and isolated populations. In the past, if patients from this sector of society needed hospitalization, institutions built with Hill-Burton funds were required to provide a designated amount of "charity care" to those in need.

In some instances, hospitals continue to follow this procedure. However, access to these alternate, less expensive types of healthcare is becoming more difficult. Cuts in government support for health programs for the poor, for persons receiving Medicare or Medicaid benefits, are making it increasingly more difficult for people who need healthcare to receive it.

Today we seem to have three tiers of care: standard care for the insured, partial care for Medicaid patients, and emergency care only for the 35 million Americans who are uninsured. Do we nurture and protect life when there appears to be an unjust distribution of the goods entrusted to our stewardship? How can Catholic hospitals continue both to survive and to implement a preferential option for the poor?

This is not merely a theological or pastoral issue. Access to standard healthcare is largely nonexistent for about half of the poor and very limited for the other half who are eligible for Medicaid or Medicare. The United States has the worst record on healthcare of any nation in the North Atlantic community and even worse than some underdeveloped nations.

Judith Feder and Jack Hadley, currently co-directors of the Center for Health Policy Studies at Georgetown University, have conducted research on uncompensated hospital care. Some of their findings are particularly disturbing. They concluded, for example, that *nonprofit* hospitals—including Catholic facilities—do very little more for the poor than *for-profit* hospitals (which is very little, indeed). Free care provided by private, nonprofit hospitals averaged only 3.85 percent of all charges (gross revenues) in 1982. I am aware that some dispute the accuracy of these findings in regard to Catholic hospitals, but I have not yet seen data which shows that, overall, these institutions provide substantially more free care than their counterparts.

Today we seem to have three tiers of care: standard care for the insured, partial care for Medicaid patients, and emergency care only for the 35 million Americans who are uninsured.

I must also affirm, of course, that there are some inner-city and other Catholic hospitals which do a great deal for the poor. Nonetheless, as the research seems to indicate, hospitals average less than five percent of patient charges for uncompensated care. Much of this is for deliveries to women who appear in heavy labor at our emergency rooms and the subsequent neonatal intensive care for their infants born with severe problems because of the lack of care given their mothers during pregnancy.

Our national resources are limited, but they are not scarce. As a nation we spend *more* per capita and a *higher* share of our Gross Domestic Product (GDP) on health than any other country in the world—nearly twice as much as Great Britain, for example. Yet our system still excludes at least half the poor. In 1982 the U.S. share of GDP devoted to healthcare was 10.6% against 5.9% within the United

Kingdom, which has universal access to healthcare and a lower infant mortality rate than the U.S.

The basic problem of healthcare in the U.S. is managerial: the effective allocation and control of resources. The key is the underlying philosophy and sense of mission which motivates and informs managerial decisions.

> *The basic problem of healthcare in the U.S. is managerial: the effective allocation and control of resources.*

As a nation, we spend enormous amounts of money to prolong the lives of newborns and the dying while millions of people don't see a doctor until they are too ill to benefit from medical care. We allow the poor to die in our hospitals, but we don't provide for their treatment in the early stages of illness—much less make preventive care available to them.

These facts are disturbing to anyone who espouses the sacredness and value of human life. The fundamental human right is to life—from the moment of conception until death. It is the source of all other rights, including the right to healthcare. The consistent ethic of life poses a series of questions to Catholic healthcare facilities. Let me enumerate just a few.

- Should a Catholic hospital transfer an indigent patient to another institution unless superior care is available there?
- Should a Catholic nursing home require large cash deposits from applicants?
- Should a Catholic nursing home transfer a patient to a state institution when his or her insurance runs out?
- Should a Catholic hospital give staff privileges to a physician who won't accept Medicaid or uninsured patients?

If Catholic hospitals and other institutions take the consistent ethic seriously, then a number of responses follow. All Catholic hospitals will have outpatient programs to serve the needs of the poor. Catholic hospitals and other Church institutions will document the need for comprehensive prenatal programs and lead legislative efforts to get them enacted by state and national government. Catholic medical schools will teach students that medical ethics includes care for the poor—not merely an occasional charity case, but a commitment to see that adequate care is available.

If they take the consistent ethic seriously, Catholic institutions will lead efforts for adequate Medicaid coverage and reimbursement policies.

They will lobby for preventive health programs for the poor. They will pay their staffs a just wage. Their staffs will receive training and formation to see God "hiding in the poor" and treat them with dignity.

I trust that each of you has an opinion about the importance or viability of responses to these challenges. My point in raising them is not to suggest simplistic answers to complex and difficult questions. I am a realist, and I know the difficulties faced by our Catholic institutions. Nonetheless, I do suggest that these questions arise out of a consistent ethic of life and present serious challenges to healthcare in this nation—and specifically to Catholic healthcare systems.

Medical ethics must include not only the "classical" questions but also contemporary social justice issues which affect healthcare. In a 1983 address to the World Medical Association, Pope John Paul II pointed out that developing an effective medical ethics—including the social justice dimension—

> fundamentally depends on the concept one forms of medicine. It is a matter of learning definitely whether medicine truly is in service of the human person, his dignity, what he has of the unique and transcendent in him, or whether medicine is considered first of all as the agent of the collectivity, at the service of the interests of the healthy and well-off, to whom care for the sick is subordinated.

He went on to remind his listeners that the Hippocratic Oath defines medical morality in terms of respect and protection of the human person.

The consistent ethic of life is primarily a theological concept, derived from biblical and ecclesial tradition about the sacredness of human life, about our responsibilities to protect, defend, nurture, and enhance God's gift of life. It provides a framework for moral analysis of the diverse impact of cultural factors—such as technology and contemporary distribution of resources—upon human life, both individual and collective.

The context in which we face new healthcare agendas generated both by technology and by poverty is that the Catholic healthcare system today confronts issues both of survival and of purpose. How shall we survive? For what purpose? The consistent ethic of life enables us to answer these questions by its comprehensiveness and the credibility which derives from its consistent application to the full spectrum of life issues.

CHAPTER 5

The Consistent Ethic of Life and the Witnesses of Catholic Healthcare

Catholic Medical Center,
Jamaica, NY, May 16, 1986

The very mention of Bhopal or Chernobyl sends shudders through people everywhere. Although the tragic deaths and injuries caused by the Bhopal disaster were confined to a particular area, its repercussions still are being felt worldwide. The Chernobyl incident, however, affects the planet more directly; the potential spread of radioactivity is even more worrisome.

These two disasters highlight a fact that has enormous significance for the future of the world community: the growing interdependence of contemporary life—an interdependence accelerated by the rapid development of science and technology—and the competition for limited natural resources. The problems and challenges of the human family today are enormously complex, increasingly global, and ominously threatening to human life and society. Each of them has moral and religious dimensions because they all affect human life.

It is crucial, therefore, that we develop a method of moral analysis comprehensive enough to recognize the linkages among the issues confronting us, yet respecting the individual nature and uniqueness of each. One approach to the broad spectrum of life issues I have called the "consistent ethic of life." In applying this ethic to healthcare systems and the issues they face, it first is important to understand its relationship to Catholic social teaching.

Two truths about the human person form the basis of Catholic social teaching: human life is both sacred and social. Because God's gift of life is sacred, we have a duty to protect and foster it at all stages of development, from conception to natural death, and in all circumstances. Because we acknowledge that human life is also social, society must protect and preserve its sanctity.

Precisely because life is sacred, the taking of even one human life is a momentous event. Traditional Catholic teaching has allowed the taking of

Published originally in *Health Progress*, July-August 1986, and in *Consistent Ethic of Life*, Sheed & Ward, Kansas City, MO, 1988.

human life in particular situations by way of exception, as, for example, in self-defense and capital punishment. In recent decades, however, the presumptions against taking a human life have been strengthened and the exceptions made more restrictive.

Fundamental to these shifts in emphasis is a more acute perception of the many ways in which life is threatened today. War, aggression, and capital punishment are not new; but today there is a new context that must be considered. This new context shapes the content of one's ethic of life.

Modern technology is the principal factor responsible for this new context. Technology induces a sharper awareness of the fragility of human life. Pope John Paul II, speaking with young people in Ravenna, Italy, May 11, 1986, acknowledged that technical progress makes it possible "to transform the desert, to overcome drought and hunger, to lighten the burden of work, to resolve problems of underdevelopment, and to render a more just distribution of resources among people of the world." But he also warned that the same technology has brought us to see "the land uninhabitable, the sea unserviceable, the air dangerous, and the sky something to fear."

The discovery of nuclear energy, for example, is one of the century's most important scientific developments. Besides its benefits to the human family, however, we have become painfully aware of its potential to destroy life. Similarly, while modern medical technology opens new opportunities for care, it also poses new threats to life, both immediate and potential. The extraordinary technological development of this century has brought with it a qualitatively new range of moral problems.

Technology must not be allowed to hold human beings as hostages. The essential questions we face are these: in an age when we *can* do almost anything, how do we decide what we *should* do? In a time when we can do almost anything *technologically*, how do we decide *morally* what we should not do?

Asking these questions along the whole spectrum of life from conception to natural death creates the need for a consistent ethic, for the spectrum cuts across such issues as genetics, abortion, capital punishment, modern warfare, and the care of the terminally ill. Admittedly each of these is a distinct, enormously complex problem, and each deserves individual treatment. No single answer and no simple response will solve all these problems. But they are linked. Moreover, we face new challenges in each of these areas. This combination of challenges cries out for a consistent ethic of life.

Society desperately needs an attitude or climate that will sustain a comprehensive, consistent defense and promotion of life. When human life is considered "cheap" or easily expendable in one area, eventually nothing is held as sacred and all lives are in jeopardy. The purpose of proposing the need for a consistent ethic of life is to argue that success on any one of the life-threatening issues is directly related to the attitude society generally holds toward life. Attitude is the place to root an ethic of life because, ultimately, it is society's attitude—whether one of respect or nonrespect—that determines its policies and practices.

Society desperately needs an attitude or climate that will sustain a comprehensive, consistent defense and promotion of life.

There is also a relationship between "right to life" and "quality of life" issues. For example, if one contends that the right to life of every unborn child should be protected by civil law and supported by civil consensus, then our moral, political, and economic responsibilities do not stop at the moment of birth. We must defend the right to life of the weakest among us; we must also be supportive of the quality of life of the powerless—the old and the young, the hungry and the homeless, working mothers and single parents, the sick, the disabled, and the dying. The viability and credibility of the "consistent ethic" principle depend primarily upon the consistency of its application.

Such a quality-of-life posture translates into specific political and economic positions—on tax policy, generation of employment, welfare policy, nutrition and feeding programs, and healthcare, for example. Consistency means we cannot have it both ways: we cannot urge a compassionate society and vigorous public and private policy to protect the rights of the unborn and then argue that compassion and public and private programs for the needy undermine society's moral fiber or that they are beyond the proper scope of government or that of the private sector. Neither can we do the opposite!

Ordinary Versus Extraordinary Procedures

The consistent ethic of life poses a challenge to two kinds of problems. The first are "classical" medical ethics questions, which today include revolutionary techniques ranging from genetics to the prolonging of life. How do we define the problems, and what does it mean to address them from a Catholic perspective?

One of the critical moral questions today is the appropriate use of ordinary and extraordinary medical procedures, especially in the care of the terminally ill.

Two fundamental principles guide discussion of these issues. The first is the principle that underlies the consistent ethic: life itself is of such importance that it is never to be attacked directly. That is why the Second Vatican Council taught: "All offenses against life itself, such as murder, genocide, abortion, euthanasia, or willful suicide . . . all these and the like are criminal; they poison civilization"("Pastoral Constitution on the Church in the Modern World," *Vatican Council II*, vol. 1, Austin Flannery, OP, ed., Costello Publishing Co., Northport, NY, 1975, para. 31).

Consequently, even in situations when a person has definitively entered the final stages of the dying process or is in an irreversible coma, it is not permitted to act directly to end life. In other words, euthanasia—intentionally causing death whether by act or omission—is always morally unjustifiable.

The second guiding principle is this: life on this earth is not an end in itself; its purpose is to prepare us for a life of eternal union with God. Consistent with this principle, Pope Pius XII ("Anesthesia: Three Moral Questions," address to the Ninth National Congress of the Italian Society of Anesthesiology, Feb. 24, 1957) gave magisterial approval to the traditional moral teaching of the distinction between ordinary and extraordinary forms of medical treatment. In effect, this means that a Catholic is not bound to initiate, and is free to suspend, any medical treatment that is extraordinary in nature.

But how does one distinguish between ordinary and extraordinary medical treatments? One first should note that the Catholic heritage does not use these terms in the same way they might be used in the medical profession. That which is judged ethically as extraordinary for a given patient can and often will be viewed as ordinary from a medical perspective because it is ordinarily beneficial when administered to most patients. Nevertheless, it is possible to define, as Pope Pius XII did, what would ethically be considered as extraordinary medical action: namely, all "medicines, treatments, and operations which cannot be obtained or used without excessive expense, pain, or other inconvenience or which, if used, would not offer a reasonable hope of benefit."

This distinction was applied by the Congregation for the Doctrine of the Faith to the care of the terminally ill in its *Declaration on Euthanasia* (U.S. Catholic Conference, Washington, DC, 1980, p. 10), which states: "When inevitable death is imminent in spite of the means used, it is permitted in conscience to take the decision to refuse forms of treatment that would only secure a precarious and burdensome prolongation of life, so long as the normal care due the sick person in similar cases is not interrupted." In other words, although the Catholic tradition forcefully rejects euthanasia, it also would argue that no obligation exists, in regard to care of the terminally ill, to initiate or continue extraordinary medical treatments that would be ineffective in prolonging life or that would, despite their effectiveness, impose excessive burdens on the patient.

The American Medical Association's Council on Ethical and Judicial Affairs recently adopted a policy statement on withholding or withdrawing life-prolonging medical treatment. Earlier this year the National Conference of Commissioners on Uniform State Laws adopted a "Uniform Rights of the Terminally Ill Act" for proposed enactment by state legislatures. Although it contains some helpful insights, the latter document raises serious moral questions that could result in ethically unsound legislative efforts, further undermining the right to life and the respect for life in American society.

In addition, certain cases involving seriously ill patients have received a good deal of media attention. In light of all this, serious reflection is needed on the question of society's ethical responsibilities to the dying.

The consistent ethic of life will prove useful in such reflection. First, an attitude of disregard for the sanctity and dignity of human life is present in society both in relation to the end of life and its beginning. Some are more concerned about whether patients are dying fast enough than whether they are being treated with the respect and care demanded by the Judeo-Christian tradition.

To counteract this mentality and those who advocate so-called mercy killing, society must develop attitudes, policies, and practices that guarantee the elderly and the chronically and terminally ill the right to the spiritual and human care they need. The process of dying is profoundly human and should not be allowed to be dominated by purely utilitarian, cost-benefit considerations.

Euthanasia—intentionally causing death whether by act or omission—is always morally unjustifiable.

Second, regarding the manner in which we care for a terminally ill person, we must incorporate the Christian belief that in death "life is changed, not ended." The integration of such a perspective into a profession whose avowed purpose is the preservation of life will not be easy. Likewise, it will be difficult for a dying person's family and loved ones to accept the fact that someone they love is involved in a process that is fundamentally good—the movement into eternal life.

By insisting on the applicability of the principle of the dignity and sanctity of life to the full spectrum of life issues and by taking into consideration the impact of technology, the consistent ethic provides additional insight to the new challenge that "classical" medical ethics questions face today. It enables defining the problems in a broader, more credible context.

Health Care for the Poor

The second challenge that the consistent ethic poses concerns "contemporary" social justice issues related to healthcare systems. The primary question is, how does the Gospel's preferential option or love for the poor shape healthcare today?

Some regard the problem as basically financial, as a question of resource allocation. A serious difficulty today is the fact that many persons are left without basic healthcare, while large sums of money for exceptional, expensive measures are invested in the treatment of a few. Although technology has provided the industry with many diagnostic and therapeutic tools, their inaccessibility, cost, and sophistication often prevent wide distribution and use.

Government regulations and restrictions, cutbacks in health programs, and the maldistribution of personnel to provide adequate services are some of the factors that contribute to the reality that—unless attitudes, policies, and programs are changed—many persons probably will not receive the kind of basic care that nurtures life.

A significant factor affecting the quality of healthcare in the United States today is the lack of medical insurance. The American Hospital Association estimates that nearly 33 million persons have no medical insurance. This number includes the 60 percent of low-income persons who are ineligible for Medicaid; nearly one-half of the "working poor;" the unemployed, seasonally employed, or self-employed; and middle-income individuals denied coverage because of chronic illnesses. They include disproportionate numbers of young adults, minorities, women, and children.

Between 1980 and 1982 the number of poor and near poor people without health insurance increased 21 percent. During the same period, free hospital care increased by less than 4 percent. According to the most recent federal data, only one-third of the officially poor are eligible for the Medicaid "safety net." The Children's Defense Fund estimates that two-thirds of poor or near-poor children are never insured or are insured for only part of the year. Some 40,000 infants die each year in the United States and others are kept alive by surgery and technology—only to die in their second year of life. The principal causes are well-known: poverty and lack of adequate medical care. Moreover, many argue that the situation worsens as hospitals become more competitive and prospective pricing holds down the reimbursement rate.

Patient "dumping" is also a concern. According to the results of a study of 467 patients transferred to Cook County Hospital in Chicago in a 42-day period in late 1983, the primary reason for a majority of transfers was economic rather than medical. And at least one-fourth of the patients were judged to be too unstable to be transferred.

In addition, only 6 percent of the patients had given written informed consent for transfer; 13 percent of the patients transferred were not informed before the transfer. When the reason for the transfer was given, the patient often did not receive the same explanation that was given to the resident physician at Cook County Hospital during the transfer request phone call.

Although each hospital must examine its own policies and practices in regard to uncompensated care of the poor, some recent studies suggest that such care of itself may not be an effective substitute for public insurance. In Arizona, for example—the only state without Medicaid—the proportion of poor Arizona residents denied care for financial reasons was about twice that of residents in states with Medicaid programs. On the other hand poor elderly Arizona residents—covered by Medicare—were found to have access to healthcare comparable to that of other states.

These facts are disturbing to anyone who espouses the sacredness and value of human life. The fundamental human right is to life—from the moment of conception until natural death. It is the source of all other rights, including the right to healthcare. The consistent ethic of life poses a series of questions and challenges to Catholic healthcare facilities.

- Should a Catholic hospital transfer an indigent patient to another institution unless superior care is available there?
- Should a Catholic nursing home transfer a patient to a state institution when his or her insurance runs out?
- Should a Catholic hospital give staff privileges to a physician who won't accept Medicaid or uninsured patients?

If Catholic hospitals and other institutions take the consistent ethic seriously, then a number of responses will follow. All Catholic hospitals will have outpatient programs to serve the needs of the poor. Catholic hospitals and other Church institutions will document the need for comprehensive prenatal programs and lead legislative efforts to get them enacted by state and national government. Catholic medical schools will teach students that medical ethics includes care for the poor—not merely care for an occasional charity case but a commitment to ensure that adequate care is available.

If they take the consistent ethic seriously, Catholic institutions will lead efforts for adequate Medicaid coverage and reimbursement policies. They will lobby for preventive health programs for the poor.

The fundamental human right is to life—from the moment of conception until natural death.

To face these challenges successfully, Catholic healthcare institutions, with the dioceses in which they are located, must collaborate in new and creative ways—ways that might have been considered impossible or undesirable before.

In short, today's agenda for Catholic healthcare facilities is new. The context in which we face this agenda is also new because, unlike the past, the Catholic healthcare system today confronts issues of survival and of purpose. The consistent ethic, primarily a theological concept derived from biblical and ecclesial tradition about the sacredness of human life and about our responsibilities to protect, defend, nurture, and enhance the gift of God, provides a framework within which we can make a moral analysis of the various cultural and technological factors that affect human life. Its comprehensiveness and consistency in application will provide both guidance and credibility and win support for our efforts. The challenge to witness to the dignity and sacredness of human life is before us. With God's help and our own determination, I am confident that we will be equal to it.

Chapter 6

Building Bridges: Collaboration in a Time of Crisis

Catholic Health Assembly,
San Diego, CA, June 4, 1986

Healthcare has been and will always be an essential component of the Church's mission. Caring for the sick, both personally and collectively through Catholic healthcare facilities, is integral to the Church's ministry. The U.S. bishops in their pastoral letter, *Health and Health Care*, affirm this commitment: "We pledge ourselves to the preservation and further development of the rich heritage that is embodied in the Church's formal health apostolate.... We commit ourselves to do our part in maintaining and developing a Catholic institutional presence within the healthcare field in our country."

What are the implications of this statement? If healthcare is an essential element of the Church's mission, how should the whole Church be involved in healthcare ministry? What roles should the various members of the Church—laity, religious, clergy, and bishops—play in such a ministry? How does reading the "signs of the times" tend to shape that ministry today?

The historical development of U.S. Catholic healthcare services and the changes occurring today put these questions into a broader context.

Historically, the Church has supported a healthcare ministry primarily through various healthcare facilities. Religious institutes (congregations) often provided the impetus for Catholic hospitals in this country. In many instances, these religious institutes saw the need for healthcare in a specific area or among particular immigrants. To respond to this need, the religious sought the diocesan bishop's approval to initiate a healthcare ministry within his diocese. Sometimes the bishop invited the religious to establish such a facility. Most bishops still view Catholic hospitals as indispensable to the Church's mission of service.

In the past, each healthcare facility operated more or less on its own. Its relationship with the local diocese, for example, usually consisted of adherence to Catholic moral principles, provision of chaplains, and the bishop's occasional visit to celebrate a special occasion. This relationship

Published originally in *Health Progress*, September 1986.

seemed suitable at the time. Catholic facilities flourished, serving all patients, regardless of race, religion, or socioeconomic status.

The healthcare scene, however, has changed dramatically in recent years. Everyday we see the difficulties Catholic facilities face because of limited resources, lower patient census, DRGs, the expense of advanced technology, and other circumstances. As a result of media exposure and marketing programs, the general public is very aware that hospitals are vigorously competing for healthcare business.

This crisis may have arisen because healthcare is being identified more and more as a "growth industry" or an "investment opportunity." How will we be able to remain faithful to our concept of mission and service in such an environment? How will we be able to balance a commitment to providing healthcare for the poor with the need for cost containment? The Catholic Health Association (CHA) Task Force on Healthcare of the Poor has articulated clearly and forcefully in its report, *No Room in the Marketplace: The Healthcare of the Poor*, released in June 1986, the impact of these changes. (See *Health Progress*, July-August 1986, pp. 87-99.)

Recently a prominent physician wrote to me in anticipation of this address and stated: "The hard financial issues faced by our institutions are forcing us to choose between ministry and economic pressure. The choice of money over ministry will ultimately lead to either the loss of a sense of mission and ministry, or a significant perversion of the meaning of these terms." He then reflected on the concomitant crisis in Catholic healthcare, its service to the poor: "When mission and ministry are subverted to technologic competitiveness and financial survival, it is this population [the poor] that falls through the cracks."

In short, Catholic healthcare is in crisis. The battle for its very soul is being waged. We are at a fork in the road, and we must make critical decisions.

However, I see the current situation as an opportunity for new growth, as a challenge to realize more fully than ever the Church's healing mission. Although I share your anxieties, I do not despair; in fact, I am optimistic. First, God has entrusted this mission to the Church, and he always gives us what we need to carry out our responsibility. Second, we have incredibly valuable human resources within the Church. All we need is to tap our creative potential to solve problems. We must pool our creative resources and energies. We must work together to do what we cannot accomplish alone.

Collaboration, not Competition

Today, with the greater awareness of healthcare as a ministry of the entire Church and with the severe crisis threatening individual facilities, my basic thesis is that collaboration rather than competition will make the difference between survival and demise. It will provide the catalyst that brings about new growth.

Collaboration is implicit in Gospel values. When Jesus prayed at the Last Supper for those who would be his future followers, he did not pray that they would be successful or even happy. Instead, he prayed that they might be one so that the world might believe the Gospel. Through collaborative efforts we can give witness that we are a living community based on a common faith, common values, and a common mission.

Many facilities have already begun to collaborate with others. New hospital systems, systems of hospital systems, and joint ventures are forming. These relationships tend to strengthen each partner's position, enabling it to fulfill its mission better and serve its people more effectively. When making such choices and decisions, however, facilities must consider the potential harm to other facilities in the area that share the same ecclesial mission.

Collaboration does not imply dispensing with all competition. Competition is healthy when it provides an incentive to be dissatisfied with oneself, to improve, and to excel. Such competition can lead healthcare providers to excellence, and this benefits the persons they serve. Competition is morally unacceptable, however, when it is dishonest or when its primary purpose is to eliminate or destroy others. The basic motivation, if we are to preserve our values and purpose of existence, must be the health and well-being of those we serve.

> *In short, Catholic healthcare is in crisis. The battle for its very soul is being waged.*

Within the Catholic healthcare apostolate, diverse talents and the differing vocations of the religious, the laity, and the ordained provide an excellent opportunity to witness to the Church Jesus prayed for. In other words, even if no particular crisis were facing Catholic healthcare today, the time would still be ripe for collaboration because the Second Vatican Council has inaugurated a renewal in Church life and ministry.

Let us now consider some changes and challenges facing three actors in the Church's health ministry: the religious, the laity, and the pastors of the Church.

Role of the Religious

As I noted earlier, the extensive Catholic healthcare system owes its existence primarily to the religious institutes (congregations) that founded them. Today most Catholic acute care hospitals remain under the sponsorship of religious institutes. These institutes have enriched the Church with their diversity, number, and dedicated service.

Although the decline in numbers of religious is undeniable, it would be a tragic loss to the Church and its health apostolate if the religious' unique witness completely disappeared. Religious have left everything to follow Christ, reminding others that something exists beyond the "here and now." They show how to glorify God through selfless service to the human family's deepest needs.

The primary responsibility to provide long-term direction to Catholic facilities and to ensure their mission effectiveness belongs to the sponsoring body. In most cases, this is a religious institute. This sponsorship is the element that endures over the years despite changes in personnel and administration. The continuing and deeper involvement of many sponsors in directing their facilities is an encouraging sign for the future of Catholic healthcare.

Religious community leaders still have many concerns. Their responsibilities often extend beyond the individual institution to include other ministries to which the institute is committed. They cannot neglect the well-being of the entire religious institute and its members. On the other hand, chief executive officers (CEOs), whether religious or lay, necessarily focus their attention on their own institution's good.

Although sponsors' and administrators' differing priorities at times may cause tensions, open communication about the institution's mission needs and its business exigencies can lead to a healthy balance between Christian ministry and financial viability.

Another hopeful sign for Catholic healthcare's future is the increasing effort to promote cooperation and collaboration among religious institutes, which often have more in common than they at first may think. Even though a founder's special charism shapes each institute, all are firmly rooted in the one Christ. A Chinese proverb says: "One moon shows in every pool; in every pool the one moon." Although every pool, pond, and puddle is different, a single light source is reflected many times. Likewise, the one Christ is reflected in every person, even though each is different. No one, either individually or as a community, can fully or perfectly mirror the Lord. His gifts and charisms are meant to be shared with others. They are not in competition but are eminently complementary.

Catholic facilities' mission statements typically express or allude to the unique charism that motivates the sponsoring religious institute. Their stated purposes share common elements, for example, in such concepts as Jesus' healing mission, the sacredness of life, care for the total person, adherence to Catholic ethical standards, a concern for social justice, and a special love for the poor. What each Catholic hospital shares with all the others—its Catholic vision of mission and service—provides the basis and the motivation for taking steps toward working together more closely. With these common elements as building blocks, we can begin to erect bridges between and among religious communities.

Another hopeful sign for Catholic healthcare's future is the increasing effort to promote cooperation and collaboration among religious institutes.

Role of the Laity

Along with the role of the religious, who play such a significant role in Catholic healthcare, we also must affirm the laity's legitimate and needed role.

Although a lay apostolate has existed in the Church since its beginning, the Second Vatican Council gave it new emphasis and importance. Two apostolic realms exist for the layperson: the secular world and the Church. The world, the marketplace, if not the laity's exclusive area, is certainly their primary responsibility. They must participate in healthcare endeavors other than Catholic-sponsored ones, bringing Gospel values and the principles of ethics and social justice to these settings. They also, however, have an indispensable role within Church institutions, which I concentrate on here.

Although the laity have always worked with religious in Catholic hospitals, only more recently have they assumed leadership in administration and governance. Whatever the reasons for this development, Catholic healthcare ministry clearly must continue to promote lay and religious collaboration.

Briefly, the layperson's unique expertise and insight is indispensable for effective ministry and for a more perfect reflection of the whole Church. Sometimes people mistakenly think that the mission aspects of healthcare are the responsibility of the religious and the clergy, and the business aspects, the laity's responsibility. The integration of both aspects is essential for both religious and laity.

Continuing education and formation in spirituality, theology, and faith development, however, are necessary to make this integration possible. Although religious have had intensive Christian formation within their institutes, laypersons often have not had similar opportunities. Retreats, value-oriented seminars, and educational programs in the Catholic healthcare philosophy can build bridges toward mutual understanding.

Organizations, such as the Academy of Catholic Healthcare Leadership, can strengthen Catholic healthcare ministry through their members' education and formation. The report of the CHA Task Force on Healthcare of the Poor recommends that the CHA develop "a seminar on the spirituality, mission, and ethical concerns involved in service of the poor" for use by sponsoring groups, systems, and local facilities. This would help to indoctrinate board members and employees.

Catholic healthcare facilities will survive and increase to serve future generations only if their leadership thoroughly understands Catholic healthcare philosophy and is committed to it as a vital Church ministry. The formation of lay leadership becomes even more essential as we explore lay sponsorship models as alternatives to more traditional Catholic healthcare sponsorship.

Role of the Church's Pastors

Although I primarily refer to bishops here, I include all clergy under the rubric of "pastors."

Because religious communities sponsor most Catholic hospitals, bishops are sensitive to their autonomy and responsibilities. At the same time, because these facilities provide healthcare within the local communities, bishops also play an important role in helping institutions carry out their individual missions.

The bishop is the Church's leader, spokesperson, and representative in his region. His responsibility, however, is not to control but "to foster the various aspects of the apostolate within his diocese and see to it that within the entire diocese or within its individual districts all the works of the apostolate are coordinated under his direction, with due regard for their distinctive character" (revised *Code of Canon Law*, c. 394).

Although he may not interfere in the internal affairs of a religious institute or its institutions, the bishop must be solicitous in matters that involve works of the apostolate. In institutional planning and expansion or curtailment of services, communication and consultation with the bishop can offer another perspective to meeting community needs.

Because healthcare is so vital to the Church's overall mission, the bishop exercises moral leadership when he facilitates a continued

Catholic presence in the provision of high-quality healthcare for those who need it, including the poor. Especially where several Catholic facilities are located in a city or metropolitan region, we must find ways to translate dreams and concerns about cooperation and collaboration into reality.

The report of the CHA Task Force on Healthcare of the Poor strikes me as a document of uncommon vision and realism. Detailing the increasingly difficult problems surrounding indigent persons' accessibility to adequate healthcare, the report recommends a plan of action that includes greater cooperation among healthcare providers, Church agencies, and government to ensure all citizens the right to healthcare. Through efforts such as these, we are building bridges consistent with and faithful to our mission.

Creative Problem Solving in Chicago

Some of the initiatives taken in the Archdiocese of Chicago illustrate the feasibility of creative solutions to the problems facing healthcare.

This past Sunday I attended the dedication ceremonies of the Howard Area Center of St. Francis Hospital. This represents a collaborative venture between St. Francis Hospital in Evanston, IL, and the Howard Area Community Center in Chicago. Its purpose is to provide healthcare and education for the many poor persons in the area, especially newly arrived Spanish-speaking immigrants.

Loyola University of Chicago recently sponsored a symposium, "Limited Resources and Commitment to the Poor," in response to my address "The Consistent Ethic of Life and Healthcare Systems" at the Foster McGaw Triennial Conference in May 1985. During the symposium the executive dean of the Stritch School of Medicine raised the possibility, among others, of Loyola's establishing a community-based, primary care satellite clinic in Maywood, one of the poorer Chicago suburbs.

In the past two years, we have been developing an area ministry in Englewood, an inner-city neighborhood. Because poverty is widespread in the area, the 10 Catholic parishes devote considerable resources to social services. In addition to a Catholic hospital within its boundaries, Englewood also has a clinic staffed by volunteers at St. Basil's parish and a primary healthcare center run by the Alexian Brothers at Our Lady of Solace parish. After two years, the St. Basil operation has serviced between 5,000 and 6,000 persons. The Our Lady of Solace center has been operating less than a year but has served about 500 people in the past three months.

Motivated by my own concern for Catholic healthcare's future viability, over a year ago I called together the CEOs at 23 Catholic hospitals in the archdiocese, along with representatives from 16 religious institutes that sponsor them. Our purpose was to discuss how joint effort and collaboration would strengthen our position and thus our mission, in a highly competitive environment.

Catholic healthcare facilities will survive and increase to serve future generations only if their leadership thoroughly understands Catholic healthcare philosophy and is committed to it as a vital Church ministry.

The participants agreed to undertake a professional study to ascertain interest in joint action and to chart possible directions for the future. On the basis of interviews with the CEOs, the provincials, archdiocesan officials, and several respected healthcare experts, the study advocated a change. It indicated that to continue a "business as usual" approach would bring far greater risks than the new model it was proposing. No change would weaken the competitive business position of existing Catholic hospitals in the archdiocese and diminish their capacity to fulfill their mission. Several hospitals would be eliminated, one by one, usually in the city's poorer section. To minimize these risks, the report recommended the development of several formalized structures for joint action that would support Catholic hospitals' charitable and business outreach.

These structures will establish a new network involving the hospitals, the sponsors, and the archdiocese and making possible joint action aimed at improving the hospitals' market competitive positions, promoting governance continuity, and ensuring maximum mission effectiveness.

Although full acceptance of all this study's recommended actions is not yet definitive, the consensus is to pursue the recommendations and take steps toward implementation. Since many persons are involved, time is needed to implement this collaborative effort fully. I have no intention of turning back, and I am confident that most of the others involved feel the same.

Face Challenges Together

These are a few examples of current efforts that one archdiocese has undertaken. The task before us throughout this nation is enormous, but

I am convinced that we have the motivation, creativity, and collective strength to see Catholic healthcare through this time of change and crisis. I also firmly believe that collaboration, difficult as it may be, is the key to Catholic health facilities' survival and growth. Collaboration strengthens the weaker institutions and benefits the Church's entire healthcare apostolate.

No one has all the answers to the complex problems that face healthcare providers today. Now is the time for all those who have a stake in and a responsibility for Catholic healthcare—religious, laity, and pastors—to join together. We must face the challenges together if we are to strengthen and expand the compassionate healing work that we do in Jesus' name.

CHAPTER 7

AIDS and Public Policy: A Church Response

American Medical Association,
Chicago, April 21, 1987

I am deeply grateful for the invitation to participate in this important conference on "AIDS and Public Policy." I commend the American Medical Association for sponsoring it and all of you for participating.

This afternoon I will speak about (1) the Catholic Church's response to AIDS; (2) the Church's call for full, human-spiritual development in the face of the AIDS crisis; and (3) finally, I will address a specifically controverted point, namely, "safe sex."

Before I begin, may I say parenthetically that at one time I intended to be a physician. It was only after I had completed the first year of college that I decided to study for the priesthood. Ministry and medicine are both noble professions. In many ways they complement one another because both are concerned with the well-being of the human person who cannot be divided into neat, totally separate compartments. Nonetheless, they approach the same reality from distinct perspectives. It is important that we keep this in mind as we dialogue about how we should address one of the most deadly diseases of our time.

1. The Catholic Church's Response to AIDS

Before I speak of the Church's response to AIDS, I want to clarify some terminology. When the medical community deals with AIDS or ARC, it does so on two fronts: *treatment* and *prevention*. Treatment is the *post factum* response. Prevention is the anticipated response. Because prospects for treatment have been so dismal, emphasis—and hope—have focused more on prevention.

The Catholic tradition understands and deals with AIDS and other similar realities in an analogous way. The Church offers a compassionate, pastoral response to individuals who have been affected by AIDS or ARC, as well as their families and friends. And in regard to those who have *not* been touched by the disease, the Church in its solicitude offers a call to full, human-spiritual development. Both approaches are similar to the medical effort to treat and prevent disease.

Let me now outline the Church's pastoral response to persons who have contracted AIDS. I will simply highlight some of its major components. Last October I issued a pastoral statement entitled *A Challenge and a Responsibility* which delineated the response of the Catholic Church in Chicago to the AIDS crisis. More recently, the Catholic bishops of California published a similar pastoral statement entitled "A Call to Compassion." Both are available to the public, and I commend them to you.

When the Church calls people to full human-spiritual development, it calls them to live out their sexuality in loving and life-giving ways.

The Church's pastoral response can be summarized in four points. Its ministry in this instance is to be seen as part of a broader healing process. Through this ministry, the Church also seeks to shape attitudes about AIDS and human behavior.

First, the Church calls all people to be loving, compassionate, and non-judgmental when dealing with persons with AIDS or ARC and their families and friends. There is no room for condemnation in this approach.

Second, the Church calls people to care for persons with AIDS in every way possible. This implies a genuine commitment, both individually and collectively, and an investment of effort and resources.

Third, the Church calls everyone to resist all discrimination against people with AIDS. They do not surrender their rights and dignity because they have contracted the disease. This applies to *all* who are affected by AIDS—adults as well as children and the unborn.

Fourth, the Church calls people to dispel panic and hysteria in dealing with AIDS. The Church encourages a study and communication of the facts and a rejection of the myths.

Our pastoral approach, and the attitudes it seeks to inculcate, addresses the medical community in a direct and relevant way. In it, healthcare and pastoral care workers will find support, affirmation, and encouragement for their important work. The Church's response also speaks to the broader community. And, to the extent that it addresses society persuasively, it will impact the formation of public policy in such areas as the allocation of funds for treatment, research, and legal efforts to prevent discrimination and harassment.

2. The Call for Full, Human-Spiritual Development

I would now like to speak about the second dimension of the Church's ministry which, in fact, is part of its teaching mission: the Church's call to full, human-spiritual development. As I indicated earlier, this is analogous to preventive medicine.

The issues here are delicate and controversial but need, nonetheless, to be addressed. I will speak clearly and without hesitation about the values and convictions of the religious tradition which I represent. I hope that I will be heard accurately.

Obviously, my brief presentation cannot encompass every specific application of the Church's teaching to all possible human behavior. Particular responses must, indeed, be particular, that is, considered and offered in an individual context. The same is true, of course, in the practice of medicine.

I also wish to emphasize that the entire direction and motivation of the Church's call to full, human-spiritual development stems from its loving solicitude for those who would place themselves or might be placed in danger of contracting AIDS, namely IV drug users, children, the unborn, and persons involved in physically and spiritually dangerous forms of homosexual and heterosexual contact. In other words, the primary concern is the well-being of people, not their condemnation however much we may disagree with their actions.

So, when the Church calls people to full, human-spiritual development, it calls for the release of people from the strangling grip of drug abuse whose basic causes must be attended to. When people's lives are devoid of meaning, they often turn to drugs. Both the Church and society need to address this. We must help people realize that, whatever their circumstances, God's gift of life is precious, and there is more to life than its sometimes superficial and depressing externals. When people find themselves in oppressive and despair-inducing poverty, again they frequently turn to drugs. Both the Church and society need to address such issues of economic well-being. The Catholic bishops recently did this in their pastoral letter on the U.S. economy, in which they asked these fundamental questions:

> What does the economy do *for* people?
>
> What does the economy do *to* people?
>
> How do people *participate* in it?

When the Church calls people to full human-spiritual development, it calls them to live out their sexuality in loving and life-giving ways. It helps to shape attitudes by recalling and applying insights and values from the Scriptures, its religious tradition, and a philosophy of the human person that is consonant with both. That is why it teaches that the normative way for living out one's sexuality is in a monogamous, heterosexual relationship of lasting fidelity in marriage. In today's culture this needs to be stated with clarity and without ambiguity.

I acknowledge, as the medical profession must also do, that such a general statement does not cover all the *de facto* variations in the human condition, variations which need individual attention. Nor does this statement about marriage propose a universal or absolute pattern for all human beings. For example, in our tradition religiously motivated celibacy is seen as an uncommon but special and appropriate way of living out one's sexuality in a loving and life-giving way. Having said that, however, I *am* affirming that marriage and family life form the foundation of our society.

In calling people to full, human-spiritual development, whether in reference to the use of drugs or the exercise of sexuality, the Church is helping to shape people's attitudes. It addresses people who are deciding how they will order their lives. It speaks also to the broader community and hopes that its voice will impact public policy in such a way that it will reflect the values of human freedom and dignity.

These comments may seem somewhat abstract in the face of an acutely distressing and concrete reality such as AIDS. So permit me to concretize the issues by discussing a controversial approach to prevention.

3. The Issue of "Safe Sex"

The point in question is the promotion of "safe sex" (as commonly understood and debated today) as a means of preventing the spread of AIDS. Coupled with this proposal is the hope (expressed by some, at least) that the Church will join in promoting "safe sex" as a preventive measure. Implicit in this hope seems to be the readiness to blame the Church for the continued spread of AIDS if it does not adopt this strategy for prevention in its educational endeavors and its ministry to persons in high-risk groups.

I must tell you that, as a pastor and a teacher, I cannot support the prevention of AIDS by promoting "safe sex" in educational programs as a solution to the spread of AIDS—any more than I could support prevention of the disease by promoting "safe drug abuse." Such an approach, while it may sincerely seek to prevent the spread of AIDS, contradicts the values embodied in the Church's call to full, human-spiritual development which I have just outlined. As such, it has no place in any educational and formational efforts.

The matter is somewhat different in regard to responses to situations where individuals have already been exposed to the disease or are likely to be exposed to it. In such cases, without compromising the values mentioned above, we have to face difficult and complex issues of public policy. The thought of St. Thomas Aquinas might provide assistance in this regard. For example, he allowed for the civil regulation of already extant brothels for the greater common good, but he certainly did not condone fornication, adultery, prostitution, and pandering. Still less would he have suggested the *establishment* of public brothels for the good of the public order.

At the same time, I would like to raise a question which seems to be rarely asked. How safe is "safe sex"? Indeed, how safe is it physically, psychologically, and spiritually?

I leave it to medical experts to answer that question at the physical or biological level. However, my impression is that, physically, "safe sex" is not inevitably and absolutely safe. Indeed, at times, it may not be safe at all.

I leave it to psychologists to consider the matter from their proper perspective. However, from the Church's experience in providing pastoral care to people for centuries, we know that full, human-psychological development is ultimately impeded and wounded by a series of momentary couplings apart from the larger, normative context which I briefly described earlier.

Finally, from a spiritual perspective, if we believe in a destiny for the human person that is deeper and more profound than what we can immediately see, hear, smell, taste, and touch, then there are many fragile, transcendent values that are not safe—indeed, they are in jeopardy—with "safe sex."

Let me express it more directly. I do not think—and I believe that our religious tradition and history sustain this—that rhetoric can reshape reality, even with a seemingly benign or comforting turn of phrase, such as "safe sex."

At best, "safe sex"—in the context in which it is being discussed—refers to "safer" not truly "safe" sexual activity. And the "safer" refers only to its physical dimension, not the psychological or spiritual. "Safe sex" offers a false sense of security, promoted no doubt in part by commercial interests and a national mentality that has sadly come to rely on "quick fixes" for profoundly human and complex issues that require more substantive and reflected solutions.

Thank you for listening to my perspective. As I said earlier, ministry and medicine, while speaking from different perspectives, are interested in and committed to the same reality—the promotion of the integral well-being of the human person. It is good for us to come together in this way, so that we can share our convictions, our hopes, our doubts, our concerns. With good will and a commitment to continue the conversation, good things can happen. May the God who is our origin and destiny guide us on paths that will lead to full human development—physically, psychologically, and spiritually.

Chapter 8

Crossroads for Church's Healthcare Ministry

National Conference of Catholic Bishops, Washington, DC, November 15, 1992

My task is to address the topic, "The Role of the Bishop in Promoting Catholic Healthcare Ministry." In reflecting on my own experience in Chicago, I am sure that I have some things in common with everyone here. First, I am very proud of the Church's healing ministry and very grateful to those who have shaped, are the leaders of, and continue to serve in this remarkable apostolate. Our Catholic healthcare system is the largest private system serving millions of people in the U.S. annually through almost 600 hospitals, more than 1,000 long-term care facilities, and many other health services. These institutions and many professional schools owe their existence to the inspiration and commitment of generations of women and men religious whose congregations sponsored and staffed them.

We have a long history of quality and professionalism, serving the sick, enhancing human dignity, and advocating better healthcare for the poor in this country. Our health apostolate is one of the finest achievements of the Church in the United States. All of us must be committed to its future vitality and progress in the face of trends which create new problems and opportunities for this essential ministry.

A part of me looks at these growing challenges in healthcare and says, "Somebody else had better worry about this. My days are already filled with addressing many other issues." But that is not a workable or realistic attitude. The vitality of our healthcare ministry must be a priority for the whole Church, and, as bishops, we cannot evade our role in meeting these challenges.

The history of the Catholic health apostolate is long, rich, and complex. It is as old as the parables of Jesus, as traditional as the corporal works of mercy, and as contemporary as MRIs, DRGs, and the national debate over healthcare reform. However, with changes in healthcare and religious life, as well as other factors, we are at a crossroads in the way we carry out the Church's healthcare ministry. In some cases, traditional models need to be renewed and reshaped to meet new realities in our

Published originally in *Origins*, vol. 22, no. 24, November 26, 1992.

Church and healthcare system. We may need new forms of governance, new models of service delivery, and new ways of collaborating to ensure that our Catholic values, presence, and identity continue to be reflected in healthcare. As bishops, we cannot ignore these realities or wait until the crisis is more acute before we join with others to meet these challenges.

In my role as a local bishop, teacher, and pastor, I have convened Catholic healthcare providers around these and other common interests through our own archdiocesan Catholic Health Alliance for Metropolitan Chicago. Some of my experiences have been successful. For example, in the northwest quadrant of the archdiocese, there was only one physician willing to serve in primary care to over 5,000 residents in need of welfare level medical service. Most of the service was delivered through hospital emergency rooms. Five Catholic hospitals came together with Catholic Charities of the archdiocese to form a physician referral network. Eventually other non-sectarian hospitals joined in the effort. Today there are over 380 doctors delivering quality primary care to individuals and families at the welfare level in that part of the archdiocese. Recently, the Catholic Health Association bestowed an award upon this creative service.

While much has been done to enhance service in the archdiocese through the Catholic Health Alliance, we are still struggling unsuccessfully to put together an instrumentality to assist hospitals where religious congregations are no longer able to sustain them or finances are threatening their closure. This is a task that calls for a solution in many of our dioceses.

There is some uncertainty or ambiguity about the bishop's role in healthcare. Most dioceses are deeply involved in healthcare. A few dioceses own and operate hospitals, clinics, and other facilities. More often, though, religious communities have generously and skillfully provided healthcare in the Church's name. In these cases, the bishop's role is less clear, and he is probably less involved. We often seek to support the ministry of others rather than exercise it ourselves. While we have our traditional canonical, pastoral, and educational responsibilities, we often serve more as convener, "cheerleader," or advocate than as decisionmaker in this area. When we do address questions of Catholic identity, our interest is sometimes perceived as interference, or our respect for autonomy as indifference or lack of concern.

On the other hand, bishops may misread recent calls for greater episcopal involvement as implying future organizational and fiscal responsibilities that are not necessarily intended. Moreover, the relationships between bishops and healthcare sponsors and leaders are sometimes affected by broader forces at work in the Church—including debates over the role of women, the future of religious life, and Church teaching on human life and sexual morality.

We need to move beyond confusion over roles to a common commitment to shape a vital future for our healthcare apostolate. Questions are being raised which go to the very heart of the Church's healing mission:

> How should the Church express its health ministry in the future?
>
> How should the Church deal with modern ethical dilemmas in a pluralistic and sometimes hostile society?
>
> How can the Church help infuse the systems which provide health services in our society with Christian values?

We have a variety of challenges: the implications of declining numbers of religious, issues of coordination and collaboration, reduced resources, and national healthcare reform.

First, a major challenge before us is the decline in the numbers of women and men religious who have historically owned and governed the majority of Catholic health facilities. This situation makes it increasingly difficult for many congregations to provide the leadership necessary to ensure the viability of their healthcare ministries. The Church must recognize that the future of the health ministry depends on creative, committed leadership, and learn how to prepare persons for leadership in a deliberate and focused way. This decline in the number of religious also raises serious questions about the continuing sponsorship of Catholic healthcare institutions by religious congregations. We need to ask:

Catholic hospitals are sometimes not seen as related to the local church in vital ways.

> As sponsorship by religious congregations is transferred to other congregations or to non-Catholic entities, how can authorization by and accountability to the Church be maintained? What are the forms that these new sponsorships will take?

Second, there has been an increasing fragmentation of community responsibility for healthcare. Catholic hospitals are sometimes not seen as related to the local church in vital ways. The average Catholic too often has little sense of health ministry as part of the Church's total mission. The relationship between bishops and the sponsors and administrators of

Catholic institutions within their dioceses is often characterized by personal warmth and good will, but too often not real collaboration until it is too late. We may fail to communicate about issues of mutual concern and accountability until a crisis is apparent.

Tensions for bishops arise from the absence of an ongoing relationship with sponsors and administrators of Catholic institutions. A growing reality is that many of the Catholic hospitals are owned and managed by a national network of a religious community. While we recognize the effectiveness and efficiency of multi-institutional systems, their structures too often contribute to distant relationships with the local church and the diocesan bishop.

A third challenge involves the new cutbacks in public funding and aggressive cost containment by both public and private healthcare purchasers. This fiscal crisis has led to less financial solvency for healthcare institutions and sharply reduced the historic cost-sharing by which health providers subsidized uncompensated care. Within this fiscal environment, Catholic hospitals are less and less able to oppose the prevailing trends and maintain a commitment to the sponsor's values, such as providing healthcare to the poor and the uninsured. The relationships between local Catholic hospitals are sometimes characterized by competition rather than cooperation. This attitude makes it difficult for a bishop, concerned about the overall issues of the Catholic healthcare ministry, to work effectively with competing sponsors and institutions during difficult financial times, or when confronted with ethical dilemmas.

The fourth challenge involves the role of bishops in healthcare advocacy. Our country has entered a debate about whether and how to reform its healthcare system in order to deal with growing problems of inadequate access, increasing costs, and quality of care, especially for poor families and children. The unrestrained escalation of healthcare costs has spawned an unprecedented problem of coverage and access. Americans without health insurance now number close to 40 million. An almost equal number have inadequate insurance. Nearly three-quarters of the uninsured are full-time workers and their families. Most disturbing of all, there are 11 million children among the uninsured. Despite huge expenditures, first-class technology, and an excellent medical education system, serious questions persist about the quality of healthcare in the United States. The symptoms of a failing healthcare system are everywhere: an unconscionable rate of infant mortality, increased malnutrition, increasing numbers of sick and homeless.

This is now a new issue for the Church. We have advocated comprehensive reform for more than two decades. We bring several essential perspectives to the discussion—as defenders of human life and human dignity, providers of healthcare, purchasers of insurance coverage for our employees, and as a community that serves and advocates for the poor and vulnerable. We must bring a constructive and distinctive voice to this debate at both the state and the national levels.

The role of the bishops is central in the light of the challenges facing Catholic healthcare ministry at this time of immense change. The significance of healing ministry in the overall mission of the Church demands the commitment of episcopal leadership. We must move now in a dramatic fashion to ensure the continued vitality of Catholic healthcare ministry. Bishops must participate to ensure the continuing Catholic identity, the commitment to the poor, and the connection to the Catholic community. We must participate to ensure that our healthcare ministry practices what we preach about human life, human dignity, the rights of workers, and the common good. Several questions provide focus to the task before us:

> How can bishops be involved and informed on relevant trends and issues in the health ministry?
>
> How can Catholic lay men and women be challenged to greater responsibility for their role in this ministry, and to demonstrate their personal commitment to its continued presence and vitality?
>
> How can bishops implement effective programs of advocacy on behalf of issues?

Conclusion

In these days of change and stress, there is simply no substitute for stronger relationships and greater collaboration between bishops and the leaders of Catholic healthcare. We need more dialogue—nationally and locally—about how we work together to enhance and preserve the Catholic commitment to healthcare. We also need to stand together in advocating national reform of healthcare which will protect and enhance the life and dignity of all our citizens, especially the poor and vulnerable.

I trust that these workshops and the other initiatives of the Catholic coalition will lead bishops to be more engaged and involved in our health ministry, and the Catholic community to be more committed to Jesus' command to heal the sick, care for the weak, and serve the least among us.

Chapter 9

The Right to Healthcare: A Test and an Opportunity for the Catholic Community

National Conference of Catholic Bishops,
Chicago, May 11, 1993

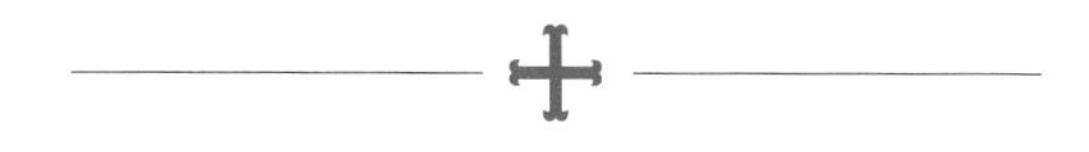

I. Introduction

I've been asked to address the social justice dimensions of the healthcare debate. As pastors, we see this question most clearly in human terms. The statistics cited this morning have names and faces for us. In Chicago, they are thousands of children without care, poor communities without adequate health services, and Catholic hospitals in neighborhoods where the option for the poor can lead to financial disaster.

Let me tell you the story of David Murillo who is nearly 22 months old. More than two years ago, when David's parents discovered they were expecting a baby, they faced a crisis. They both worked, but had no health insurance. They were ineligible for public aid because of their income. Their values told them to seek life, not an abortion. Fortunately, they learned about the Maternity Fund—a wonderful partnership forged among Catholic hospitals, dedicated doctors, and the Archdiocese of Chicago. David's parents contacted the Fund and were sent to St. Mary of Nazareth Hospital where his mother became a patient of Dr. Seong Soo Lee, a doctor who has taken care of more than 40 similar cases. The doctor reduced his fees; the hospital contributed many of the other costs for prenatal care and delivery; and the archdiocese provided the rest of the needed funding so that David could be born as a healthy child.

This story of a family in need is repeated many times over in every diocese in this country. David and his family deserved more than the ingenuity and charity provided by the Maternity Fund. They have a *right* to decent healthcare, and so does every individual, regardless of his or her circumstances.

As Catholic bishops, our pastoral urgency is reenforced by a heritage of moral reasoning that guides our contribution to the healthcare debate. This debate is not only an issue of political, economic, and social significance for the nation; it is also a time of testing and a moment of opportunity for the Church. We will be tested on how our teaching contributes to the moral framework for reform. Our tradition can illuminate important aspects of the debate, illustrating the potential of the Catholic social vision on contemporary issues.

II. Framing the Argument: Healthcare, Common Good, & Social Justice

A. ***The Right to Healthcare*** is the starting point of the moral argument in Catholic social teaching. Our teaching that human life must be protected and human dignity promoted leads us to insist that people have a right to healthcare since its absence can destroy the life and dignity of the human person. This right is explicitly affirmed in *Pacem in Terris*, but it is not defined in specific terms. In the U.S. debate, it is our task as teachers of the Church to fill out the meaning of Pope John XXIII's assertion, and, indeed, our episcopal conference has sought to do this over the years in a number of ways. We have used the consistent ethic of life to frame the larger discussion. More specifically, the conference, in a letter last year from Bishop Malone to members of the U.S. Congress, outlined eight basic criteria for healthcare reform.

Healthcare meets all of the essential criteria of a right, i.e., a moral claim to a *good*, essential for human dignity. We insist that a basic floor of healthcare must be available to all persons.

When over 37 million Americans are without health coverage, when rising costs threaten the coverage of millions more, when infant mortality remains shockingly high, the right to healthcare is seriously undermined, and our healthcare system is in need of serious reform.

B. ***Common Good***: It is best to situate the need for healthcare reform in the context of the common good—that combination of spiritual, temporal, and material conditions needed if each person is to have the opportunity for full human development.

The right to healthcare is a constitutive element of the common good. Failure to secure this right leads not simply to declining protection of human dignity, but can lead to the loss of life—the basis of human dignity. For example, in one recent year 40,000 children died before their first birthday, in large part because of the lack of access to prenatal care. This link between healthcare and the common good is a critical need and an elusive challenge in a debate likely to be dominated by powerful, special interest lobbies, political action committee (PAC) contributions, and partisan goals.

The duty to create the conditions for the common good rests upon society as a whole, but no single element of society has total responsibility for the common good or, in this case, for healthcare. The duties are manifold:

1. *The duties of individuals*: Every right presupposes a duty; the duty incumbent upon each individual is to exercise proper stewardship of one's health.

2. *The duties of the healthcare professions*: Using the principle of subsidarity, Catholic teaching turns first to the healthcare professions as having a primary responsibility for meeting healthcare needs. It is now abundantly clear that the healthcare professions cannot meet this need alone, so both the principles of subsidiarity and the idea of socialization (cf. *Mater et Magistra*, 1961) require going beyond the professions.

3. *The duties of government*: The requirements of providing healthcare today demand a role for government. Subsidiarity *first* demands that other agencies be designated as the source of healthcare. The same principle (subsidarity), supplemented by socialization and solidarity (cf. *Centesimus Annus*), demands the involvement of the state as the guarantor of basic healthcare for each person. In Catholic teaching the state has positive moral responsibilities for the common good, and particular responsibilities for those most in need in society.

Healthcare is a basic good which should be guaranteed (at some decent and defined level) for each member of society. The ultimate (but not sole) guarantor is the government. It can fulfill this responsibility in multiple ways (e.g., taxation, powers of regulation, establishment of standards of care, and levels of eligibility, as well as assisting individuals in securing care.)

The existing patterns of healthcare in the United States do not meet the minimal standard of social justice.

C. ***Healthcare and Social Justice***: Since society as a whole is responsible for meeting the healthcare needs of its citizens, healthcare must be justly ordered if rights are to be protected, duties appropriately allocated, and the demands of the common good met.

The existing patterns of healthcare in the United States do not meet the minimal standard of social justice. The substantial inequity of our healthcare system can no longer be ignored or explained away. The current healthcare system is so inequitable, the disparity—between rich and poor, between the sick and the well, and between those with access and those without—is so great, that it is clearly unjust. The principal defect is that a significant part of the society (37 million) do not have a guaranteed access to basic healthcare. Others have some access, but their coverage is too limited or too costly to offer health security for their families.

Traditional Catholic doctrine on distributive justice and the common good, as well as more contemporary teaching on the option for the poor and the imperatives of solidarity, points to a special obligation to meet the healthcare needs of the poor and the unserved. In our pastoral letter on the economy, we insist that the poor have the single, most urgent, moral claim on the policies of the nation. Personal and institutional decisions, policies of private and public bodies, must be evaluated by their effects on those who lack the minimum necessities, including healthcare. When we enter the public arena, our judgments should be based primarily on what public policy will mean for the poorest and most vulnerable in society.

As has been already suggested, *discrimination* exacerbates the injustice within our health system. African-Americans and Hispanics are disproportionately uninsured. Many of the 40,000 who die before their first birthday are minority children. Black mothers are three times as likely to die of preventable complications of pregnancy as white mothers.

Since this system consumes a seventh of our national economic resources, a Catholic approach to reform should reflect the traditional virtue of *stewardship*. We call for cost controls, not only to eliminate duplication and waste, but also to free up resources for other vital national needs.

In summary, the Catholic case for reform begins with the right to healthcare, focuses on the common good and social justice, and reflects the virtues of solidarity and stewardship. Our teaching tradition leads to the kind of criteria outlined by our conference and the urgency for reform that brings us here today. We seek a system which will ensure access for all, contain costs, respect pluralism, and enhance human life and human dignity.

III. Other Essential Moral Issues in the Policy Debate

Our task will be made much more complex and challenging by the likelihood that the proposal presented to Congress will include abortion as one of the basic healthcare services to be provided all citizens. Depending on the actual design of the proposal, this can seriously affect the participation of Catholic healthcare institutions in the new system and, indeed, their very survival.

So, the question arises, how do the social justice themes I just described relate to other moral principles? Catholic concerns about healthcare go beyond (but never away from) its character as an issue of justice, and these concerns should never be seen as being in conflict with, or contradicting, each other. Since there are moral demands in both areas, it is crucial that both be maintained in any final position we take as a conference.

How will we respond, then, as a conference, if the proposed plan includes abortion as a basic healthcare service?

We will be able to affirm the basic elements of the plan, while working, as we have in the past, to exclude abortion from the mandated services. We have more than enough arguments to sustain this position. Our primary objective should be a policy which seeks justice across the spectrum of life: legislation which excludes abortion (justice for the unborn) and guarantees healthcare (justice from birth to natural death). The best method of securing both of these goals is a federal policy which meets both criteria. At the same time, we should also advocate the inclusion in any legislation of conscience clauses that will protect the beliefs and convictions of individual healthcare workers and healthcare institutions which, by corporate identity, are opposed to abortion.

If this proves impossible at the national level, a secondary method might be to replace a national mandate with provisions that permit states to decide whether abortion is included in a healthcare package. Since most states have chosen not to fund abortion, this may be an alternative to explore.

What if some of our objectives are met in a bill, but not others? Obviously the specifics of this case would have to be known in detail before one could make a clear moral judgment. We do not face these ethical challenges empty-handed. We have a religious and theological heritage of reflection on how we maintain our ethical identity in a world of conflicting values. The difficulty is that these principles were developed in a very different socio-economic environment. In large measure, they were intended to guide the decisions of individuals. Today, the challenge is to relate these principles to institutions that are either an expression of the Church's official ministry or are related to that ministry in a complex social and economic environment. And, to be candid, we have found ourselves in disagreement about the application of these very same principles in recent years.

In our response to the proposed reform, we will also build coalitions with other people of good will in order to achieve our objective of a reformed healthcare system that protects the dignity of human life from conception to natural death. Some will agree with us in our efforts to protect the life of the unborn, but will not agree with our other commitments. As a conference, we must continue to point out that a positive moral vision sustains our commitment to the poor, our commitment to the dignity of the human person (including the right to adequate healthcare), as well as our commitment to the life of the unborn. If we do not do this, we will give the pro-abortion movement ample grounds to cast us in a narrow, sectarian, and elitist perspective.

IV. Conclusion

The current healthcare system is failing to nurture the full health of the American people and the common good of our society. The present moment presents a unique opportunity when true reform of this unjust and unsustainable healthcare system seems a realistic possibility. Under these circumstances, we have an obligation to work for fundamental reform of healthcare, to achieve a system which fosters respect for all human life and human dignity.

We will need both moral wisdom and political skill to advance our values in a political environment often hostile to both the unserved and the unborn. Some say the choice is clear: Pursue healthcare reform without regard for the anti-life dimensions of possible legislation. Others say: Oppose healthcare reform if it includes abortion. Both of these strategies are inadequate. Both groups are too ready to accept defeat and call it victory.

Attempts to link public funding of abortion with national healthcare do not serve the best interests of our nation and would be a tragic setback. So, too, would the demise of genuine healthcare reform be a tragic outcome for tens of millions of Americans. If we work as hard as we can, but cannot prevail on the abortion issue in this political climate, are we morally compelled to help defeat much needed healthcare for poor families and vulnerable children? Such an outcome would be not only a defeat for a piece of vital legislation, but a loss for our Church and a serious setback for our social tradition. I hope we can find in our community the political resources to avoid this nightmare, if at all possible. I pray we will find in our moral tradition the ethical principles to guide us through this terrible dilemma, if it proves necessary. In this regard, we need to involve in our deliberations theologians as well as the religious who sponsor and administer Catholic healthcare institutions.

What is really at stake in this case is not simply politics or principles, but the lives and dignity of millions of our sisters and brothers. Healthcare is a matter of fundamental justice, because, for so many, it is literally a matter of life and death, of lives cut short and dignity denied.

Chapter 10

The Consistent Ethic of Life and Healthcare Reform

National Press Club,
Washington, DC, May 26, 1994

As many of you may know, in the last year I have experienced a significant amount of press coverage for reasons that are happily behind me. There is a temptation in this prestigious forum to share some of my reactions and reflections based on that experience, but I am going to resist that temptation. At another time and after more reflection on my part, I might share some thoughts about what I learned about the news media and related topics. But today I address a more important and more timely topic—the moral dimensions of healthcare reform.

For the last decade as a pastor, a bishop, and a leader of our National Conference of Catholic Bishops, I have had the opportunity to address a series of vital moral challenges. I chaired the committee that produced the pastoral letter on war and peace a decade ago. I have served as chair of our bishops' committees on pro-life matters and family-life concerns. As a bishop, I have also seen the crime, injustice, and violence in our neighborhoods and the loss of roots and responsibility in our cities, the loss of the sense of family and caring in our communities that is undermining millions of lives.

I believe that at the heart of so many of our problems—in Chicago and Washington, in Bosnia and Rwanda—there is a fundamental lack of respect for human life and human dignity. Over the past 10 years I have articulated a "Consistent Ethic of Life" as a moral framework to address the growing violence in our midst.

The purpose of the consistent life ethic is to provide a moral framework for analysis and motivation for action on a wide range of human life-issues with important ethical dimensions. The consistent life ethic, by design, provides for a public discourse that respects the separation of church and state, and also recognizes the proper role of religious perspectives and ethical convictions in the public life of a pluralistic society.

Over the past years I have addressed many issues in the light of the consistent ethic. In addition to the central question of abortion, I have

Published originally in *Origins*, June 9, 1994. Reprinted with permission from *A Moral Vision for America*, Joseph Cardinal Bernardin, Georgetown University Press, Washington, DC, 1998.

spoken about euthanasia and assisted suicide, capital punishment, the newer technologies used to assist human reproduction, and war and peace, to name a few. The foundation for all of these discussions is a deep conviction about the nature of human life, namely, that human life is sacred, which means that all human life has an inalienable dignity that must be protected and respected from conception to natural death. For the Christian believer and many others, the source of this dignity is the creative action of God in whose "image and likeness" we are made. Still others are aware that life is a precious gift which must be protected and nurtured.

For advocates of a consistent life ethic, the national debate about healthcare reform represents both an opportunity and a test. It is an *opportunity* to address issues and policies that are often matters of life and death, such as, who is covered and who is not; which services are included and which are not; will reform protect human life and enhance dignity, or will it threaten or undermine life and dignity? It is a *test* in the sense that we will be measured by the comprehensiveness of our concerns and the consistency of our principles in this area.

In this current debate, a consistent life ethic approach to healthcare requires us to stand up for both the unserved and the unborn, to insist on the inclusion of real universal coverage and the exclusion of abortion coverage, to support efforts to restrain rising health costs, and to oppose the denial of needed care to the poor and vulnerable. In standing with the unserved and the unborn, the uninsured and the undocumented, we bring together our pro-life and social justice values. They are the starting points for a consistent life agenda for healthcare reform.

In these remarks I speak as a pastor of a diverse local church. In Chicago we see both the strengths and the difficulties of our current system. We experience the remarkable dedication, professionalism, and caring of the *people* and the amazing contributions of the *institutions* that make up our healthcare system. I also see the children without care, the sick without options, the communities without adequate health services, the families and businesses strained and broken by healthcare costs. We see the hurts and pick up the pieces of a failing system—in our hospitals and clinics, our shelters and agencies, our parishes and schools. We look at healthcare reform from the bottom up, not who wins or loses politically, not how it impacts powerful institutions and professions, but how it touches the poor and vulnerable, the unserved and the unborn, the very young and the very old.

As I indicated earlier, I am also a member of the National Conference of Catholic Bishops, an organization deeply involved in this debate. Our principles and priorities are summarized in a resolution unanimously adopted by the conference last year. A unanimous vote of our bishops is an unusual accomplishment, as those of you who have ever seen us discuss holy days or liturgical texts can attest! But we found unity in embracing a consistent life ethic approach to healthcare reform.

The broader healthcare debate is driven by many factors. For the sake of time, I will list only five without discussing them at any length.

> 1. The amount of money spent on healthcare is escalating at an unsustainable rate. It surpassed 14 percent of the gross domestic product (GDP) last year, and it is reasonable to assume that, without effective intervention, it could reach 18% of the GDP by the year 2000.
>
> 2. This uncontrolled growth is creating economic hardships for many of our fellow citizens, especially working families.
>
> 3. Private insurance programs are deteriorating through risk segmentation into programs that more and more serve those who have the least need for health insurance—the healthy.
>
> 4. Cost shifting—that is, the passing on of unreimbursed expenses by health providers to employer premiums—has become a "hidden tax" that no longer is sustainable.
>
> 5. Finally, and most significantly, the number of uninsured in the United States continues, now approaching nearly 40 million, a large portion of whom are people who work. Ten million are children. This lack of coverage touches African-American and Hispanic families most directly.

I join the many who have concluded that the United States needs profound systemic change in its healthcare system. We cannot rely on the system to correct itself. Without intervention, things are getting worse, not better.

For advocates of a consistent life ethic, the national debate about healthcare reform represents both an opportunity and a test.

I hasten to add that my advocacy is not partisan. Neither do I argue on behalf of any particular proposal before the Congress. I do, however, take exception with those who say that there is no serious systemic problem or that what we merely face is an insurance or a healthcare delivery problem. On the contrary, there *is* a fundamental healthcare problem in our nation today. I share this judgment with many leaders of the Catholic community whose outlook and convictions have been shaped

- by the experience of Catholic religious communities and dioceses that operate 600 hospitals and 300 long-term care facilities, constituting the largest non-profit group of healthcare providers in the United States

- by the experience of the Catholic Church in the United States, which purchases health coverage for hundreds of thousands of employees and their families

- by the experience of Catholic Charities, the largest private deliverer of social services in the nation

- by our experience as a community of faith, caring for those who "fall through the cracks" of our current system.

It is this broad range of experience that led the U.S. Catholic bishops to say last June:

"Now is the time for real healthcare reform. It is a matter of fundamental justice. For so many it is literally a matter of life and death, of lives cut short and dignity denied. We urge our national leaders to look beyond special interest claims and partisan differences to unite our nation in a new commitment to meet the healthcare needs of our people, especially the poor and the vulnerable. This is a major political task, a significant policy challenge and a moral imperative."

Before addressing some of the more specific issues associated with healthcare reform, it is important that we consider some even more profound issues. I say this because President Clinton's healthcare reform proposal and the alternatives to it, like any significant government initiatives that would reorder social relationships and responsibilities, have drawn us into a discussion of fundamental values and social convictions. Several important convictions, which serve as a kind of bedrock for the consistent life ethic, can assist us in this broader discussion. They are:

1. There are *basic goods and values* which we human beings share because we share the gift of human life; these goods and values serve as the common ground for a public morality that guides our actions as a nation and as a society.

2. Within the individual, these common goods and values express themselves in an inalienable human dignity, with consequent *rights* and *duties*.

3. One of the ways these rights and duties are expressed in the human community is through the recognition and *pursuit of the*

common good; or, to say it differently, through a good that is to be pursued in common with all of society; a good that ultimately is more important than the good of any individual.

4. This common good is realized in the context of a *living community*, which is nurtured by the virtues and shared values of individuals. Such a community protects the basic rights of individuals.

5. As part of this community, both individuals and institutions (including government, business, education, labor, and other mediating structures) have an *obligation*, which is rooted in distributive justice, to *work to secure this common good*; this is how we go about meeting the reasonable claims of citizens striving to realize and experience their fundamental human dignity.

These convictions find their origin in a vision of the human person as someone who is grounded in community, and in an understanding of society and government as being largely responsible for the realization of the common good. As Catholics we share this vision with many others. It is consistent with fundamental American values, though grounded differently. For example, our Declaration of Independence and our Constitution reflect a profound insight that has guided the development of our nation; namely, that there are certain fundamental human rights that exist before the creation of any social contract (such as the constitution of a sovereign nation), and that these must be protected by society and government. There is an objective order to which we are held accountable and to which we, in turn, hold others accountable in our many relationships and activities. The Catholic tradition also affirms such rights but sees them emerging from the organic relationship between the individual and the community.

As a nation, we also have had a sense of a common good which is greater than the agenda of any individual. Alexis de Tocqueville noted this when he commented on the American penchant for volunteering. We also have been a nation of communities. Whether in the small towns of the Plains or the ethnic communities of the large cities, U.S. citizens had a sense of being bonded together and being mutually responsible. We also recognized that our individual and collective existence is best protected by virtuous living—balancing the demands of personhood and social responsibility. In more recent years, as our social order has become more complex, we have come to see that a proper sense of mutual responsibility requires a greater presence of the state in helping individuals to realize their human potential and social responsibility. Public education and social security are but two examples of this presence.

Without being overly pessimistic, I suggest that these fundamental convictions, which are essential both to a consistent life ethic and to our well-being as a nation and a society, are being challenged today. There is abroad a certain tendency which would suggest that law and public order are accountable only to the subjective convictions of individuals or pressure groups, not to any objective, albeit imperfectly perceived, moral order. Robert Bellah and his associates have convincingly shown how a sense of the common good, the role of community, and the value of virtuous living have been compromised, if not lost, in recent years. I am convinced that the violence that plagues our nation is a symptom of this loss of an overarching social order. We are a nation that is increasingly overly individualistic at the very time when the problems we face require greater common effort and collective responses.

All of this needs to be taken into consideration in any substantive discussion of healthcare reform. If we are not attentive to issues such as these, then our dialogues and debates will go nowhere because of disagreements—unknown and unacknowledged—on basic principles.

First, there is the issue of *universal access*. In the June 1993 statement I cited earlier, the U.S. Catholic bishops outlined key principles and priorities for initiating and executing reform. Our third principle was universal access to comprehensive healthcare for every person living in the United States.

We believe that healthcare—including preventive and primary care—is not only a commodity; it is an essential safeguard of human life and dignity. In 1981, the bishops spoke of healthcare as a "basic human right which flows from the sanctity of human life." In declaring this, the bishops were not saying that a person had a right to *health*, but that, since the common good is the sum of those conditions necessary to preserve human dignity, one must have a right of *access*, insofar as it is possible, to those goods and services which will allow a person to maintain or regain health. And if one views this right within the context of the convictions I have just discussed, then it is the responsibility of society as a whole and government to ensure that there is a common social order that makes the realization of this good possible. Whether we have healthcare should not depend on whom we work for, how much our parents earn, or where we live.

Now is the time for real healthcare reform. It is a matter of fundamental justice.

So far, so good. Most would agree, at least in theory. Where the disagreement comes is in regard to the last of the convictions I noted in discussing the consistent ethic. Allow me to rephrase it.

> Under the title of distributive justice, society has the obligation to meet the reasonable claims of its citizens so that they can realize and exercise their fundamental human rights.

When many of us Americans think of justice, we tend to think of what we can claim from one another. This is an individualistic understanding of justice. But there is another American instinct which has a broader understanding of justice. It has been summarized by Father Philip Keane, a moral theologian, who wrote: "...justice shifts our thinking from what we claim from each other to what we *owe* to each other. Justice is about duties and responsibilities, about building the good community." In this perspective, distributive justice is the obligation which falls upon society to meet the reasonable expectations of its citizens so that they can realize and exercise their fundamental human rights. And, in this instance, the right is that of access to those goods and services that make it possible for persons to maintain their health and thus broaden healthcare beyond what is provided by a hospital, a clinic, or a physician.

When I speak of universal coverage, I do not mean a vague promise or a rhetorical preamble to legislation, but the practical means and sufficient investment to permit all to obtain decent healthcare on a regular basis.

So far I have argued that healthcare is an essential safeguard of human life and dignity and that there is an obligation for society to ensure that a person be able to realize this right. I now want to go a step further. I believe that the only way this obligation can be effectively met by society is for our nation to make *universal healthcare coverage* a reality. Universal *access* is not enough. We can no longer tolerate being the only Western nation that leaves millions of persons uncovered. For many, this will be a "hard saying." The cry of political expediency and the maneuvering of special interest groups already are working either to provide a program of access that maintains a two-tiered healthcare system (which marginalizes large portions of our society) or to limit coverage. When I speak of universal coverage, I do not mean a vague promise or a rhetorical preamble to legislation, but the *practical means* and *sufficient investment* to permit all to obtain decent healthcare on a regular basis.

If justice is a hallmark of our national community, then we must fulfill our obligations in justice to the poor and the unserved *first* and not last. Similarly, we cannot ignore the millions of undocumented immigrants. Even if the demands of justice were set aside, reasons of public health would necessitate their being included. The undocumented will continue to need medical assistance, and hospitals will continue to be required to provide medical care for those who present themselves for treatment. In a reformed system, which should contain, if not eliminate, the cost-shifting that previously had paid for their care, the medical expenses of the undocumented must be covered for both policy and moral reasons.

Unfortunately, as the national debate on healthcare reform has evolved, and as legislation has been proposed, an important fact has been lost; namely, that it is not enough simply to expand coverage. If real reform is to be achieved—that is, reform that will ensure quality and cost-effective care—then we must do what is necessary in order to ensure that our healthcare delivery system is person-centered and has a community focus. Healthcare cannot be successfully reformed if it is considered only an economic matter. This reform will be morally blighted if the nature of care—something profoundly human, not easily measured, yet that which, far more than technology, remains the heart and breath of the art of healing—is not preserved and expanded along with health coverage itself. The challenge is to provide universal coverage without seriously disrupting the doctor/patient relationship which is so central to good medical care.

After a long period of research and discussion, the Catholic Health Association (CHA) developed a proposal for healthcare reform that seeks to meet this and other challenges. It is called *Setting Relationships Right.* I hope that the values CHA has proposed and the strategies it has developed in this regard will not be lost sight of. Our objective must be a healthy nation where the mental and physical health of the individual is addressed through collaborative efforts at the local level.

Let me summarize my major points so far. First, we need a profound systemic reform of our healthcare system. Second, justice and the common good demand that this reform include universal coverage. Third, justice at this time requires a program of effective universal coverage that is person-centered and community-based. This leads us to two thorny questions: How is the program to be funded, and how are costs to be contained?

As you know, these two questions are essentially interrelated. It is clear that the rate of cost increases in healthcare cannot be sustained even if there is no systemic reform. It also is clear that the demands of a more fiscally responsible use of federal monies must be taken into account. We cannot spend what we do not have.

Our episcopal conference has insisted that healthcare reform must also include effective mechanisms to restrain rising healthcare costs. Without cost containment, we cannot make healthcare affordable and direct scarce national resources to other pressing national problems. Containing costs is crucial if we are to avoid dangerous pressures toward the kind of rationing that raises fundamental ethical and equity questions. The poor, vulnerable, and uninsured persons cannot be denied needed care because the health system refuses to eliminate waste, duplication, and bureaucratic costs.

But we may also have to consider other steps to restrain costs and distribute healthcare more justly. For example, we may have to recognize that basic and preventive care, and healthcare to preserve and protect life, should be a higher priority than purely elective procedures. This raises the often explosive concept of "rationing." I prefer a different word and a different concept—"stewardship." How do we best protect human life and enhance human dignity in a situation of limited health resources? How do we ensure that the lives and health of the poor and vulnerable are not less valuable or less a priority than the lives and health of the rest of us?

This is not an abstract discussion. Rationing healthcare is a regular, if unacknowledged, feature of our current healthcare system. Nearly 40 million are uninsured; 50 million more are underinsured. In 1992, nearly 10 million children were without medical coverage, 400,000 more than in 1991. In my own state of Illinois, 86,000 persons lose their health insurance each month. Being without insurance means being without care when you need it, delaying care until an illness or injury may require more costly intervention or be beyond any treatment.

We now have an insurance model that requires individuals to pay for the items and services which their healthcare needs require—some without limitations and others with enormous constraints. We have been rationing healthcare in recent years by squeezing people out of the system through insurance marketing techniques like medical underwriting, preexisting condition exclusion, and insurance red-lining. Actuarial pricing designed to protect insurance company assets pits one group against another—the old against the young, the sick against the healthy—thus undermining the solidarity of the whole community. We can see this tension playing itself out in the disturbing debates around this country about assisted suicide.

In light of these concerns, the nation must undertake a broad-based and inclusive consideration of how we will choose to allocate and share our healthcare dollars. We are stewards, not sole owners, of all our resources, human and material; thus, goods and services must be shared. This is not a task for government alone. Institutions and individuals must be involved in reaching a shared moral consensus, which will allow us to reassert the essential value of the person as an individual and as a member of the community. From that moral consensus must come a process of decision making and resource allocation which preserves the dignity of all persons, in particular the most vulnerable. It is proper for society to establish limits on what it can reasonably provide in one area of the commonweal so that it can address other legitimate responsibilities to the community. But in establishing such limits, the inalienable life and dignity of every person, in particular the vulnerable, must be protected.

We have been rationing healthcare in recent years by squeezing people out of the system through insurance marketing techniques.

CHA has addressed the ethics of rationing and offered some moral criteria. These demand that any acceptable plan must meet a demonstrable need, be oriented to the common good, apply to all, result from an open and participatory process, give priority to disadvantaged persons, be free of wrongful discrimination, and be monitored in its social and economic effects.

This kind of framework offers far better guidance than the moral bankruptcy of assisted suicide and the ethically unacceptable withhholding of care based on "quality of life" criteria. We will measure any cost containment initiative by two values: Does it distribute resources more justly? And does it protect the lives and dignity of the poor and vulnerable.

But the problem of rationed access to necessary medical care is only one aspect of the cost containment debate. What of the issue of *funding*? Obviously I cannot offer a detailed analysis of the specific proposals which are on the table. But I can say this: If systemic reform addresses in a substantive manner issues of quality care and cost effectiveness, then justice will demand that all sectors of our society contribute to the support of these efforts. And this support takes two forms. First, each individual must assume appropriate responsibility for the costs associated with healthcare, and must assume responsibility to do all that is possible not to put his or her health at risk. Second, those segments of our economic order, which have been able to avoid an appropriate level of responsibility for the healthcare of their employees, must begin to assume their fair share, just as the rest of society must. In other words, we all must be willing to help meet this demand of justice. We must share the sacrifices that will have to be made.

Thus far, I have insisted that a consistent life ethic requires a commitment to genuine universal coverage, because lack of coverage threatens the lives and diminishes the dignity of millions of men, women, and children. I must also say clearly and emphatically that a consistent life ethic requires us to lift the burden of mandated abortion coverage from needed healthcare reform. I say this for several important reasons:

> 1. It is morally wrong to coerce millions of people into paying for the destruction of unborn children against their consciences and convictions. How ironic it would be if advocates of "choice," as they call themselves, require me and millions like me to obtain and pay for abortion coverage, which we abhor. It is a denial of "choice," a violation of conscience, and a serious blow to the common good.
>
> 2. It is politically destructive. Needed national healthcare reform must not be burdened by abortion coverage, which neither the country nor the Congress supports. Public opinion polls and recent Congressional action clearly indicate that, whatever their views on the morality or legality of abortion, the American people and their representatives do not wish to coerce all citizens into paying for procedures that so divide our nation. A University of Cincinnati poll in January of this year indicated that only 30 percent favor the inclusion of abortion as a basic benefit even if it could be included at no cost at all. Only 14 percent wanted abortion coverage if it would add to the cost of health premiums.
>
> 3. Abortion mandates would undermine the participation of Catholic and other religious providers of healthcare, who now provide essential care in many of the nation's most underserved communities. I fear our hospitals will be unable to fulfill their mission and meet their responsibilities in a system where abortion is a mandated benefit. Strong conscience clauses are necessary to deal with a variety of medical/moral issues, but are not sufficient to protect Catholic and other providers who find abortion morally objectionable. The only remedy is not to link needed reform to abortion mandates.

The sooner the burden of abortion mandates is lifted, the better for the cause of reform. We continue to insist that it would be a grave moral tragedy, a serious policy mistake, and a major political error to link healthcare reform to abortion. An insistence on abortion coverage will turn millions of advocates of reform into adversaries of healthcare legislation.

We cannot and will not support reform that fails to offer universal coverage or that insists on abortion mandates. While this offers moral consistency, it can place us in conflicting political alliances. For example, we concur with the position of the President and Mrs. Clinton in calling real universal coverage essential. We concur with Representative Henry Hyde and the pro-life caucus in insisting that abortion coverage must be abandoned. We concur with the Hispanic Caucus in our commitment that universal coverage must be truly "universal coverage."

This is our consistent ethic message to the White House, the Congress, and the country. We are advocates of these key principles and priorities, not any particular plan. We will not choose between our key priorities. We will work with the leaders of our land to pass healthcare reform, reform that reflects a true commitment to human life and human dignity. As I noted above, the polls indicate that most Americans join us in support for both authentic universal coverage and the exclusion of abortion coverage in healthcare reform. We will carry this message forward with civility and consistency. We offer our moral convictions and practical experience, not political contributions and endorsements. We have no "attack ads" or PAC funds. But we can be a valuable partner for reform, and we will work tirelessly for real reform without abortion mandates.

For defenders of human life, there is no more important or timely task than offering an ethical and effective contribution to the healthcare debate. The discussions and decisions over the next months will tell us a lot about what kind of society we are and will become. We must ask ourselves: What are the choices, investments, and sacrifices we are willing to make in order to protect and enhance the life and dignity of all, especially the poor and vulnerable? In the nation's capital, healthcare reform is seen primarily as a *political* challenge—the task of developing attractive and workable proposals, assembling supportive coalitions, and securing the votes needed to pass a bill. But fundamentally, healthcare reform is a *moral* challenge—finding the values and vision to reshape a major part of national life to protect better the life and dignity of all.

We cannot and will not support reform that fails to offer universal coverage or that insists on abortion mandates.

Ultimately, this debate is not simply about politics—about which party or interest group prevails. It is about *children,* who die because of the lack of prenatal care or the violence of abortion. About *people* who have no healthcare because of where they work or where they come from. About *communities* without care, and workers without coverage.

Healthcare reform is both a *political* task and a *moral* test. As a religious community with much at stake and much to contribute to this debate, we are working for healthcare reform that truly reaches out to the unserved, protects the unborn, and advances the common good.

CHAPTER 11

Making the Case for Not-For-Profit Healthcare

Harvard Business School Club of Chicago, January 12, 1995

Good afternoon. It is a privilege to address the Harvard Business School Club of Chicago on the critical, but often conflicted issue of healthcare. Because of its central importance to human dignity, to the quality of our community life, and to the Church's mission in the world, I have felt a special responsibility to devote a considerable amount of attention to healthcare at both the local and national levels.

In the last year, I have spoken at the National Press Club on the need to ensure access to adequate healthcare for all; I have issued a Protocol to help ensure the future presence of a strong, institutional healthcare ministry in the Archdiocese of Chicago; and in order to be more in touch with ongoing developments in the field, I have joined the Board of Trustees of the Catholic Health Association of the United States—the national organization that represents more than 900 Catholic acute and long-term care facilities.

In the interest of full disclosure, I must warn you that this considerable activity does not qualify me as a healthcare expert. Healthcare policy is challenging and extraordinarily complicated, and in this area I am every bit the layman. But because of its central importance in our lives—socially, economically, ethically, and personally—we "non-experts" avoid the healthcare challenge at our peril.

I come before you today in several capacities. First, as the Catholic Archbishop of Chicago who has pastoral responsibility for numerous Catholic healthcare institutions in the archdiocese—though each is legally and financially independent. Second, as a community leader who cares deeply about the quality and availability of healthcare services throughout metropolitan Chicago and the United States. And third, as an individual who, like you, will undoubtedly one day become sick and vulnerable and require the services of competent and caring medical professionals and hospitals.

THE GROWING THREAT TO NOT-FOR-PROFIT HEALTHCARE

In each role I am becoming increasingly concerned that our healthcare delivery system is rapidly commercializing itself, and in the process is

Published originally in *Origins*, January 16, 1995.

abandoning core values that should always be at the heart of healthcare. These developments have potentially deleterious consequences for patients and society as a whole. This afternoon, I will focus on one important aspect of this problem: the future vitality and integrity of not-for-profit hospitals.

In their struggle for economic survival, a growing number of not-for-profits are sacrificing altruistic concerns for the bottom line.

Not-for-profit hospitals constitute the overwhelming majority of Chicagoland hospitals. They represent more than three quarters of the nonpublic acute-care general hospitals in the country. Not-for-profit hospitals are the core of this nation's private, voluntary healthcare delivery system, but are in jeopardy of becoming for-profit enterprises.

Not-for-profit hospitals began as philanthropic social institutions, with the primary purpose of serving the healthcare needs of their communities. In recent decades, they have become important non-governmental "safety net" institutions, taking care of the growing numbers of uninsured and underinsured persons.

Indeed, most not-for-profit hospitals regard the provision of community benefit as their principal mission. Unfortunately, this historic and still necessary role is being compromised by changing economic circumstances in healthcare, and by an ideological challenge to the very notion of not-for-profit healthcare.

Both an excess supply of hospital beds and cost-conscious choices by employers, insurers, and government have forced not-for-profits into new levels of competition for *paying* patients. They are competing with one another, with investor-owned hospitals, and with for-profit ambulatory facilities. In their struggle for economic survival, a growing number of not-for-profits are sacrificing altruistic concerns for the bottom line.

The not-for-profit presence in healthcare delivery is also threatened by a body of opinion that contends there is no fundamental distinction between medical care and a commodity exchanged for profit. It is argued that healthcare delivery is like other necessary economic goods such as food, clothing, and shelter and should be subject to unbridled market competition.

According to this view, economic competition in healthcare delivery is proposed as a welcome development with claims that it is the surest way to eliminate excess hospital and physician capacity, reduce healthcare prices, and ensure the "industry's" long-term efficiency. Many proponents of this view question the need for not-for-profit hospitals since they believe investor-owned institutions operate more efficiently than their not-for-profit counterparts and can better attract needed capital. Thus, they attack the not-for-profit hospital tax exemption as an archaic and unwarranted subsidy that distorts the healthcare market by providing exempt institutions an unfair competitive advantage.

This afternoon, I will make three arguments: first, that there is a fundamental difference between the provision of medical care and the production and distribution of commodities; second, that the not-for-profit structure is better aligned with the essential mission of healthcare delivery than is the investor-owned model; and third, that leaders in both the private and public sector have a responsibility to find ways to preserve and strengthen the not-for-profit hospital and healthcare delivery system in the United States. Before making these arguments I need to clarify an important point.

The Advantages of Capitalism and Free Enterprise

In drawing the distinction between medical care and other commodities on the one hand, and not-for-profit and investor-owned institutions on the other, I am not expressing any general bias against capitalism or the American free enterprise system. We are all beneficiaries of the genius of that system. To paraphrase Pope John Paul II: If by capitalism is meant an economic system that recognizes the fundamental and positive role of business, the market, private property, and the resulting responsibility for the means of production—as well as free human creativity in the economic sector—then its contribution to American society has been most beneficial.

As a key element of the free enterprise system, the American business corporation has proved itself to be an efficient mechanism for encouraging and minimizing commercial risk. It has enabled individuals to engage in commercial activities that none of them could manage alone. In this regard, the purpose of the business corporation is specific: to earn a growing profit and a reasonable rate of return for the individuals who have created it. The essential element here is a *reasonable* rate of return, for without it the commercial corporation cannot exist.

Society's Non-Economic Goods

That being said, it is important to recognize that not all of society's institutions have as their essential purpose earning a reasonable rate of return on capital. For example, the purpose of the family is to provide a protective and nurturing environment in which to raise children. The purpose of education at all levels is to produce knowledgeable and productive citizens. And the primary purpose of social services is to produce shelter, counseling, food, and other programs for people and communities in need. Generally speaking, each of these organizations has as its essential purpose a non-economic goal: the advancement of human dignity.

And this is as it should be. While economics is indeed important, most of us would agree that the value of human life and the quality of the human condition are seriously diminished when reduced to purely economic considerations. Again, to quote Pope John Paul II, the idea that the entirety of social life is to be determined by market exchanges is to run "the risk of an 'idolatry' of the market, an idolatry which ignores the existence of *goods which by their nature are not and cannot be mere commodities*." (Emphasis added.)

This understanding is consistent with the American experience. In the belief that the non-economic ends of the family, social services, and education are essential to the advancement of human dignity and to the quality of our social and economic life, we have treated them quite differently from most other goods and services. Specifically, we have not made their allocation dependent solely on a person's ability to afford them. (For example, we recognize that individual human dignity is enhanced through a good education, and that we all benefit by having an educated society; so we make an elementary and secondary education available to everyone, and heavily subsidize it thereafter. By contrast, we think it quite appropriate that hair spray, compact discs, and automobiles be allocated entirely by their affordability.)

Healthcare: Not Simply a Commodity

Now it is my contention that healthcare delivery is one of those "goods which by their nature are not and cannot be mere commodities." I say this because healthcare involves one of the most intimate aspects of our lives—our bodies and, in many ways, our minds and spirits as well. The quality of our life, our capacity to participate in social and economic activities, and very often life itself are at stake in each serious encounter with the medical care system. This is why we expect healthcare delivery to be a competent *and* a caring response to the broken human condition—to human vulnerability.

To be sure, we expect our physician to earn a good living and our hospital to be economically viable, but when it comes to *our* case we do not expect them to be motivated mainly by economic self-interest. When it comes to *our* coronary by-pass or *our* hip replacement or *our* child's cancer treatment, we expect them to be professional in the original sense of that term—motivated primarily by patient need, not economic self-interest. We have no comparable expectation—nor should we—of General Motors or Wal-Mart. When we are sick, vulnerable, and preoccupied with worry we depend on our physician to be our confidant, our advocate, our guide and agent in an environment that is bewildering for most of us, and where matters of great importance are at stake.

The availability of good healthcare is also vital to the character of community life. We would not think well of ourselves if we permitted healthcare institutions to let the uninsured sick and injured go untreated. We endeavor to take care of the poor and the sick as much for our benefit as for theirs. Accordingly, most Americans believe society should provide everyone access to adequate healthcare services just as it ensures everyone an education through grade twelve. There is a practical aspect to this aspiration as well because, like education, healthcare entails community-wide needs which it impacts in various ways: We all benefit from a healthy community; and we all suffer from a lack of health, especially with respect to communicable disease.

Finally, healthcare is particularly subject to what economists call *market failure*. Most healthcare "purchases" are not predictable, nor do medical services come in standardized packages and different grades suitable to comparison shopping and selection—most are specific to individual need. Moreover, it would be wrong to suggest that seriously ill patients defer their healthcare purchases while they shop around for the best price. Nor do we expect people to pay the full cost of catastrophic, financially devastating illnesses. This is why most developed nations spread the risk of these high-cost episodes through public and/or private health insurance. And due to the prevalence of health insurance, or third-party payment, most of us do not pay for our healthcare at the time it is delivered. Thus, we are inclined to demand an infinite amount of the very best care available. In short, healthcare does not lend itself to market discipline in the same way as most other goods and services.

The value of human life and the quality of the human condition are seriously diminished when reduced to purely economic considerations.

So healthcare—like the family, education, and social services—is *special*. It is fundamentally different from most other goods because it is essential to human dignity and the character of our communities. It is, to repeat, one of those "goods which by their nature are not and cannot be mere commodities." Given this special status, the primary end or essential purpose of medical care delivery should be a cured patient, a comforted patient, and a healthier community, *not* to earn a profit or a return on capital for shareholders. This understanding has long been a central ethical tenet of medicine. The International Code of the World Health Organization, for example, states that doctors must practice their profession "uninfluenced by motives of profit."

The Advantages of Not-for-Profit Institutions

This leads me to my second point, that the primary non-economic ends of healthcare delivery are best advanced in a predominantly not-for-profit delivery system.

Before making this argument, however, I need to be very clear about what I am *not* saying: I am *not* saying that not-for-profit healthcare organizations and systems should be shielded from all competition. I believe properly structured competition is good for most not-for-profits. For example, I have long contended that the quality of elementary and secondary education would benefit greatly from the use of vouchers and expanded parental choice in the selection of schools; similarly, the Catholic Health Association's proposal for healthcare reform envisions organized, economically disciplined healthcare systems competing with one another for enrollees.

Second, I am *not* saying that all not-for-profit hospitals and healthcare systems act appropriately; some do not. But the answer to this problem is greater accountability in their governance and operation, not the extreme measure of abandoning the not-for-profit structure in healthcare.

What I *am* saying is that the not-for-profit structure is the preferred model for delivering healthcare services. This is so because the not-for-profit institution is uniquely designed to provide essential human services. Management expert, Peter Drucker, reminds us that the distinguishing feature of not-for-profit organizations is not that they are non-profit, but that they do something very different from either business or government. He notes that a business has "discharged its task when the customer buys the product, pays for it, and is satisfied with it," and that government has done so when its "policies are effective." On the other hand, he writes:

"The 'non-profit' institution neither supplies goods or services nor controls (through regulation). Its 'product' is neither a pair of shoes nor an effective regulation. Its product is a changed human being. The non-profit institutions are human change agents. Their 'product' is a cured patient, a child that learns, a young man or woman grown into a self-respecting adult; a changed human life altogether."

In other words, the purpose of not-for-profit organizations is to improve the human condition, that is, to advance important non-economic, non-regulatory functions that cannot be as well served by either the business corporation or government. Business corporations describe success as consistently providing shareholders with a reasonable return on equity. Not-for-profit organizations never properly define their success in terms of profit; those that do have lost their sense of purpose.

Not-for-profit organizations never properly define their success in terms of profit; those that do have lost their sense of purpose.

This difference between not-for-profits and businesses is most clearly seen in the organizations' different approaches to decision making. The primary question in an investor-owned organization is: "How do we ensure a reasonable return to our shareholders?" Other questions may be asked about quality and the impact on the community, but always in the context of their effect on profit. A properly focused not-for-profit always begins with a different set of questions:

- What is best for the person who is served?
- What is best for the community?
- How can the organization ensure a prudent use of resources for the whole community, as well as for its immediate customers?

Healthcare's Essential Characteristics

I believe there are four essential characteristics of healthcare delivery that are especially compatible with the not-for-profit structure, but much less likely to occur when healthcare decision making is driven predominantly by the need to provide a return on equity. These four essential characteristics are:

- Access
- Medicine's patient-first ethic
- Attention to community-wide needs
- Volunteerism

Let me discuss each.

First, there is the need for access. Given healthcare's essential relationship to human dignity, society should ensure everyone access to an adequate level of healthcare services. This is why the United States Catholic Conference and I argued strongly last year for universal insurance coverage. This element of healthcare reform remains a moral imperative.

But even if this nation had universal insurance, I would maintain that a strong not-for-profit sector is still critical to access. With primary accountability to shareholders, investor-owned organizations have a powerful incentive to avoid not only the uninsured and underinsured, but also vulnerable and hard-to-serve populations, high-cost populations, undesirable geographic areas, and many low-density rural areas. To be sure, not-for-profits also face pressure to avoid these groups, but *not* with the *added* requirement of generating a return on equity.

> ***Mediating structures such as family, church, education, and healthcare are the institutions closest to the control and aspirations of most Americans.***

Second, not-for-profit healthcare organizations are better suited than their investor-owned counterparts to support the patient-first ethic in medicine. This is all the more important as society moves away from fee-for-service medicine and cost-based reimbursement toward capitation. (By "capitation" I mean paying providers in advance a fixed amount per person regardless of the services required by any specific individual.)

Whatever their economic disadvantages, fee-for-service medicine and cost-based reimbursement shielded the physician and the hospital from the economic consequences of patient treatment decisions and, thereby, provided strong economic support for a patient-first ethic in American medicine. Few insured patients were ever undertreated, though some were inevitably overtreated. Now we face a movement to a fully capitated healthcare system that shifts the financial risk in healthcare from the *payers of care* to the *providers.*

This development raises a critically important question: "When the provider is at financial risk for treatment decisions, who is the patient's advocate?" How can we continue to put the patient first in this new arrangement? This challenge will become especially daunting as we move into an intensely price competitive market where provider economic survival is on the line everyday. In such an environment the temptation to undertreat could be significant. Again, not-for-profits will face similar economic pressure but not with the added requirement of producing a reasonable return on shareholder equity. Part of the answer here, I believe, is to ensure that the nation not convert to a predominantly investor-owned delivery system.

Third, in healthcare there are a host of community-wide needs that are generally unprofitable, and therefore unlikely to be addressed by investor-owned organizations. In some cases, this entails particular services needed by the community but unlikely to earn a return on investment, such as expensive burn units, neonatal intensive care, or immunization programs for economically deprived populations. Also important are the teaching and research functions needed to renew and advance healthcare.

The community also has a need for continuity and stability of health services. Because the primary purpose of not-for-profits is to serve patients and communities, they tend to be deeply rooted in the fabric of the community and are more likely to remain—if they are needed—during periods of economic stagnation and loss. Investor-owned organizations must, on the other hand, either leave the community or change their product line when return-on-equity becomes inadequate.

Fourth, volunteerism and philanthropy are important components of healthcare that thrives best in a not-for-profit setting. As Peter Drucker has noted, volunteerism in not-for-profit organizations is capable of generating a powerful countercurrent to the contemporary dissolution of families and loss of community values. At a time in our history when it is absolutely necessary to strengthen our sense of civic responsibility, volunteerism in healthcare is more important than ever. From the boards of trustees of our premier healthcare organizations to the hands-on delivery of services, volunteers in healthcare can make a difference in peoples' lives and "forge new bonds to community, a new commitment to active citizenship, to social responsibility, to values."

Role of Mediating Institutions

In addition to my belief that the not-for-profit structure is especially well aligned with the central purpose of healthcare, let me suggest one more reason why each of us should be concerned that not-for-profits remain a vibrant part of the nation's healthcare delivery system: They are important *mediating institutions*.

The notion of mediating structures is deeply rooted in the American experience: On the one hand, these institutions stand between the individual and the state; on the other, they mediate against the rougher edges of capitalism's inclination toward excessive individualism. Mediating structures such as family, church, education, and healthcare are the institutions closest to the control and aspirations of most Americans.

The need for mediating institutions in healthcare is great. Private sector failure to provide adequately for essential human services such as healthcare invites government intervention. While government has an obligation to ensure the availability of and access to essential services, it generally does a poor job of delivering them. Wherever possible we prefer that government work through and with institutions that are closer and more responsive to the people and communities being served. This role is best played by not-for-profit hospitals. Neither public nor private, they are the heart of the voluntary sector in healthcare.

Earlier, I identified several reasons why I believe investor-owned organizations are not well suited to meeting all of society's needs and expectations regarding healthcare. Should the investor-owned entity ever become the predominant form of healthcare delivery, I believe that our country will inevitably experience a sizeable and substantial growth in government intervention and control.

Until now, I have made two arguments: first, that healthcare is more than a commodity—it is a service essential to human dignity and to the quality of community life; and second, that the not-for-profit structure is best aligned with this understanding of healthcare's primary mission. My concluding argument is that private and public sector leaders have an urgent civic responsibility to preserve and strengthen our nation's predominantly not-for-profit healthcare delivery system.

This is a pressing obligation because the not-for-profit sector in healthcare may already be eroding as a result of today's extremely turbulent competitive environment in healthcare. The problem, let me be clear, is *not* competition per se, but the kind of competition that undermines healthcare's essential mission and violates the very character of the not-for-profit organization by encouraging it—even requiring it—to behave like a commercial enterprise.

Contemporary healthcare markets are characterized by hospital overcapacity and competition for scarce primary care physicians, but also, and more ominously, by shrinking health insurance coverage and growing risk selection in private health insurance markets. These latter two features encourage healthcare providers to compete by becoming very efficient at avoiding the uninsured and high risk populations, and by reducing necessary but unprofitable community services—behavior that strikes at the heart of the not-for-profit mission in healthcare. Moreover, the environment leads some healthcare leaders to conclude that the best way to survive is to become for-profit or to create for-profit subsidiaries. The existence of not-for-profits is further threatened by the aggressive efforts of some investor-owned chains to expand their market share by purchasing not-for-profit hospitals and by publicly challenging the continuing need for not-for-profit organizations in healthcare.

ADVANCING THE NOT-FOR-PROFIT HEALTHCARE MISSION

Each of us and our communities have much to lose if we allow unstructured market forces to continue to erode the necessary and valuable presence of not-for-profit healthcare organizations. It is imperative, therefore, that we immediately begin to find ways to protect and strengthen them.

How can we do this? Without going into specifics, I believe it will require a combination of private sector and governmental initiatives. Voluntary hospital board members and executives must renew their institutions' commitment to the essential mission of not-for-profit healthcare. Simultaneously, government must reform health insurance markets to prevent "redlining" and assure everyone reasonable access to adequate healthcare services. Finally, government should review its tax policies to ensure that existing laws and regulations are not putting not-for-profits at an inappropriate competitive disadvantage, but are holding them strictly accountable for their tax-exempt status.

Let me conclude by simply reiterating the thesis I made at the beginning of this talk. Healthcare is fundamentally different from most other goods and services. It is about the most human and intimate needs of people, their families, and communities. It is because of this critical difference that each of us should work to preserve the predominantly not-for-profit character of our healthcare delivery in Chicago and throughout the country.

BIBLIOGRAPHY

Bernardin, Joseph L., "The Consistent Ethic of Life and Healthcare Reform," *Origins*, vol. 24, June 9, 1994.

Dougherty, Charles J., "The Costs of Commercial Medicine," *Theoretical Medicine*, vol. 11, 1990.

Drucker, Peter F., *Managing the Non-Profit Organization: Practices and Principles*, HarperCollins Publishers, New York, NY, 1990.

John Paul II, "Centesimus Annus," *Origins*, vol. 21, May 16, 1991.

Relman, Arnold S., "What Market Values Are Doing to Medicine," The *Atlantic Monthly*, March 1992.

Seay, David J., Vladeck, Bruce C., *Mission Matters*, United Hospital Fund of New York, NY, 1987.

CHAPTER 12

The Challenges Facing Catholic Healthcare Ministry

Catholic Conference of Illinois,
Chicago, January 13, 1995

The issues facing us in the healthcare field and the possible strategies to address them are larger than any one diocese can address effectively. That is why we felt it would be good to come together as a province or state. No healthcare institution, system, or diocese should feel alone or isolated. Moreover, because of the complex and interrelated nature of the challenges we face, it is important that you know of the solidarity of the bishops as you plan for the future.

In my remarks today, I would like to highlight three points:

1. The place of healthcare in our society
2. The importance of maintaining not-for-profit hospitals
3. The challenges facing Catholic healthcare ministry.

The Place of Healthcare in Our Society

First, what is the place of healthcare within the social order? I believe that healthcare is best understood when we use the framework of the Consistent Ethic of Life. The purpose of the consistent life ethic is to provide a moral framework for analysis and motivation for action on a wide range of human-life issues with important ethical dimensions. The consistent life ethic, by design, provides for a public discourse that respects the separation of Church and state. But it also recognizes the proper role of religious perspectives and ethical convictions in the public life of a pluralistic society.

The foundation for the consistent ethic is a deep conviction about the nature of human life, namely, that it is sacred, which means that all human life has an inalienable dignity that must be protected and respected from conception to natural death. For the Christian believer and for many others, the source of this dignity is the creative action of God in whose "image and likeness" we are made. Even many who may not have specifically religious convictions are aware that life is a precious gift which must be protected and nurtured.

A consistent life ethic approach to healthcare requires us to stand up for both the unserved and the unborn, to insist on the inclusion of real universal coverage and the exclusion of abortion coverage, to support efforts to restrain rising health costs, and to oppose the denial of needed care to the poor and vulnerable. In standing with the unserved and the unborn, the uninsured and the undocumented, we bring together our pro-life and social justice values. They are the starting-point for a consistent life agenda for healthcare in today's society.

Several important convictions, which serve as a kind of bedrock for the consistent life ethic, can assist us as we discuss healthcare. They are:

1. There are *basic goods and values* which we human beings share because we share the gift of human life; these goods and values serve as the common ground for a public morality that guides our actions as a nation and as a society.

2. Within the individual, these common goods and values express themselves in an inalienable human dignity, with consequent *rights* and *duties*.

3. One of the ways these rights and duties is expressed in the human community is through the recognition and *pursuit of the common good*; or, to say it differently, through a good that is to be pursued in common with all of society; a good that ultimately is more important than the good of any individual.

4. This common good is realized in the context of a *living community*, which is nurtured by the virtues and shared values of individuals. Such a community protects the basic rights of individuals.

5. As part of this community, both individuals and institutions (including government, business, education, labor, and other mediating structures) have an *obligation*, which is rooted in distributive justice, to work to secure this common good; this is how we go about meeting the reasonable claims of citizens striving to realize their fundamental human dignity.

These convictions find their origin in a vision of the human person as someone who is grounded in community, and in an understanding of society and government as being largely responsible for the realization of the common good.

For these reasons, we believe that healthcare—including preventive and primary care—is not merely a commodity; it is an essential safeguard of human life and dignity. That is why, in 1981, the bishops spoke of healthcare as a "basic human right which flows from the sanctity of human life." If this is so, then a person must have a right of access, insofar as it is possible, to those goods and services which one needs to maintain or regain health. And it is the responsibility of society and government to ensure that this occurs. Whether we have healthcare should not depend on whom we work for, or how much our parents earn, or where we live.

The Importance of Maintaining Not-for-Profit Hospitals

It is this perspective of healthcare that prompted me to speak yesterday about the current challenges to not-for-profit hospitals in an address to the Harvard Business School Club of Chicago.

Not-for-profit hospitals began as philanthropic social institutions, with the primary purpose of serving the healthcare needs of their communities. In recent decades, they have become important non-governmental "safety net" institutions taking care of growing numbers of uninsured and underinsured persons. Indeed, most not-for-profit hospitals regard the provision of community-benefit as their principal mission. Unfortunately, this historic and still necessary role is being compromised by changing economic circumstances in healthcare, and by an ideological challenge to the very notion of not-for-profit healthcare.

In light of this, I reaffirmed that there is a fundamental difference between the provision of medical care and the production and distribution of commodities. I then proposed that the not-for-profit structure is more in accord with the essential mission of healthcare delivery and that leaders at the community, healthcare, and governmental levels have a responsibility to promote and strengthen the not-for-profit hospital and healthcare delivery system in the United States.

Whether we have healthcare should not depend on whom we work for, or how much our parents earn, or where we live.

I further argued that, while it is appropriate that many of the institutions in our society have as their essential purpose earning a return on equity for shareholders, that need not be true of all of society's institutions.

For example, the goal of the family is to provide a protective and nurturing environment in which to raise children. The purpose of education at all levels is to produce knowledgeable and productive citizens. And the primary purpose of most social services is to provide shelter, counselling, food, and other services for people and communities in need. Generally speaking, each of these organizations has as its essential purpose a noneconomic goal: namely, the advancement of human life and dignity.

And this is as it should be. While economics is indeed important, most of us would agree that the value of human life and the quality of the human condition are seriously diminished when reduced to purely economic considerations. To quote Pope John Paul II, the idea that the entirety of social life should be determined by market exchanges is to run the "risk of an 'idolatry' of the market, an idolatry which ignores the existence of goods which by their nature are not and cannot be mere commodities."

This understanding is entirely consistent with our American experience. In the belief that the noneconomic ends of the family, social services, and education are essential to the advancement of human dignity and to the quality of our social and economic life, we have treated them quite differently from most other goods and services. Specifically, we have not made their allocation dependent solely on one's ability to afford them. (For example, we recognize that individual human dignity is enhanced through a good education, and that we all benefit by having an educated society. So, we make an elementary and secondary education available to everyone and heavily subsidize it thereafter. By contrast, we think it quite appropriate that hair spray, compact discs, and automobiles are allocated entirely by their affordability.)

Healthcare: Not Simply a Commodity

Now it is my contention that healthcare delivery is one of those "goods which by their nature are not and cannot be mere commodities." I say this because healthcare involves one of the most intimate aspects of our lives—not only our bodies, but, in many ways, our minds and spirits as well. The quality of our life, our capacity to participate in social and economic activities, and, very often, life itself, are at stake in each serious encounter with the medical care system. This is why we expect healthcare delivery to be a competent *and* caring response to the broken human condition—to human vulnerability.

To be sure, we expect our physician to earn a good living and our hospital to be economically viable, but when it comes to *our* case we do not expect them to be motivated mainly by economic self-interest. When it comes to *our* coronary by-pass or *our* hip replacement or *our* child's cancer treatment, we expect them to be professional in the original sense of that term—motivated primarily by patient need, not economic self-interest. We have no comparable expectation—nor should we—of General Motors or Wal-Mart. When we are sick, vulnerable, and preoccupied with worry, we depend on our physician to be our confidant, our advocate, our guide and agent in an environment that is bewildering for most of us, and where matters of great importance are at stake.

The availability of good healthcare is also vital to the character and well-being of our community life. We would not think well of ourselves if we permitted healthcare institutions to let the uninsured sick and injured go untreated. We endeavor to take care of the poor and the sick as much for our benefit as for theirs. Accordingly, most Americans believe society should provide everyone access to adequate healthcare services just as it ensures that everyone have an education through grade twelve. There is a practical aspect to this aspiration as well because, like education, healthcare entails community-wide needs which it impacts in various ways: We all benefit from a healthy community, and we all suffer from lack of health, especially with respect to communicable disease.

So healthcare—like the family, education, and social services—is *special.* It is fundamentally different from most other goods because it is essential to human dignity and the character of our communities. It is, to repeat, one of those "goods which by their nature are not and cannot be mere commodities."

Given this special status, the primary end or essential purpose of medical care delivery should be a cured patient, a comforted patient, and a healthier community, *not* earning a profit or a return on capital for shareholders. This understanding has long been a central ethical tenet of medicine. The International Code of the World Health Organization, for example, states that doctors must practice their profession "uninfluenced by motives of profit."

I say all of this by way of context. Even if we did not sponsor hospitals, as Catholics, we would and should be involved in the national discussion about the future of healthcare in our nation. But we do sponsor hospitals and other healthcare facilities. We do so because we believe that the provision of faith-inspired healthcare is one of the Church's ministries and is essential to the Church's life and mission. While the manner in which this ministry is exercised has changed, and will change even more, the ministry itself must continue.

Historically, this ministry has been established and carried on by women and men religious. While in some instances the diocesan bishop was actively involved in inviting a religious congregation to establish a ministry to the sick and the dying, by and large, our predecessors had little active involvement in the actual development and delivery of healthcare services. Consequently, a benign distance developed between the two. You carried on your apostolic efforts on your own, with little contact with the bishop and, perhaps, even less contact among yourselves.

In recent years, however, that has begun to change. Many diocesan bishops have sought to establish stronger pastoral ties between themselves and the healthcare ministry, and to facilitate communication and collaboration among and between those directly involved in the ministry. We have done this because it is our responsibility to do so. Healthcare *is* a ministry, and, as diocesan bishops, we share with you the responsibility of ensuring that this ministry is carried on in an effective manner. More specifically, we have the responsibility of coordinating the various components of the ministry so that it will be viable, both now and in the future.

The primary end or essential purpose of medical care delivery should be a cured patient, a comforted patient, and a healthier community, not earning a profit or a return on capital.

In doing this, however, we all have encountered numerous difficulties. Allow me to mention a few:

> The very pace of change in the so-called healthcare industry is staggering. It is not clear exactly how and where the forces of change will take us. Even the most experienced find themselves to be almost amateurs.
>
> Religious communities that established and have sustained this ministry are experiencing profound changes themselves. I do not need to elaborate on that.
>
> Another factor, difficult to hear but true nonetheless, is the fact, noted by Patricia Cahill of the New York Archdiocese, that many "Catholic sponsors don't trust one another, and that sentiment also finds expression among the managements and medical staffs of our institutions and agencies. It seems for some there is a great fear of giving something up to one another on the one hand, and the almost naive willingness to cut the same deal with a non-Catholic entity."

Nonetheless, we remain hopeful that, despite the obstacles, we can and will maintain an extensive, vibrant, fiscally sound Catholic healthcare presence in the State of Illinois and our nation. We know this will happen because you are determined to make it happen. In this rapidly changing environment, we also realize that it is unlikely that the Catholic hospitals will be able to create a vibrant network without cooperating with some non-Catholic hospitals.

Undoubtedly, there are many non-Catholic hospitals that share our values, respect our commitment to life, and will respect our efforts to promote Catholic service in healthcare. Moreover, in recent years the Church has benefitted from extensive contacts with both Christian and non-Christian denominations. We now understand much better how to work cooperatively with such groups, emphasizing our common commitments, and respecting differences. I am confident that our experience in this field will be of great benefit to our Catholic hospitals in the future.

In such collaboration, however, the assumption is that a Catholic healthcare institution will remain Catholic, in name, orientation, and operation. As noted earlier, one of our important responsibilities as diocesan bishops is to ensure and promote Catholic presence and identity in our dioceses, in the state and the nation. But there is no way that we can foster this presence and identity without the assistance of thousands of committed individuals like yourselves. But not only individuals—institutions as well. The configurations of Catholic institutions of healthcare will surely change in the years to come. But we need good, strong, identifiably Catholic institutions in healthcare. It would be a major tragedy to lose or substantially diminish an institutional identity in Catholic healthcare that has been laboriously developed since the very beginnings of Catholicism in the Midwest. And we need the courage to leave behind or radically alter those institutions or systems that no longer can carry on in an effective manner.

Healthcare is not an economic commodity; consequently, we have a responsibility to promote and strengthen the not-for-profit healthcare delivery system in the United States.

If we are to maintain our presence, it will be necessary that all of us—bishops, sponsors, administrative officers, doctors—expand our horizons and think in terms of the common good of healthcare ministry. Every decision we make must include two questions, in addition to those we normally ask about the mission and ministry needs of a particular institution or system:

1. Will this decision enhance or detract from our providing Catholic healthcare throughout the state in the future?

2. Will this decision enhance or detract from our ability to provide effective, faith-filled, quality healthcare for the poor in our state, region, and nation in the future?

All of this is by way of context for our meeting today. Allow me to draw these thoughts together. The following points are supported by all of the diocesan bishops of Illinois.

> It is our responsibility as a Catholic community, and as members of the broader society, to work together to ensure that the social order provides access to those goods and services which will allow a person to maintain or regain health.
>
> Healthcare is not an economic commodity; consequently, we have a responsibility to promote and strengthen the not-for-profit healthcare delivery system in the United States.
>
> The provision of faith-inspired healthcare is one of the Church's ministries and is essential to the Church's life and mission. Therefore, it must be promoted and strengthened in this time of profound change.
>
> For this to happen, we must leave behind past prejudices and strategies in order to enter into new patterns of collaboration as Catholic providers.
>
> Priority should be given to collaborating with Catholic partners and avoiding decisions or actions that would be inimical to the "common good" of the healthcare ministry, or would unjustly injure another Catholic institution.
>
> Collaboration with other-than-Catholic institutions should be consistent with and protective of our Catholic identity and be in accord with the best interests of the Catholic healthcare ministry, locally, regionally, and nationally.

These may seem to be almost self-evident principles to which most people would subscribe. But you know better than I that it is often difficult to implement them fully, especially when you are faced with concrete challenges and choices; and when such tremendous changes are occurring in the healthcare field that making no choice presents the greatest risk of all.

In closing, I wish—in my own name and that of all the bishops—to thank you for your dedication to the healthcare ministry. What you have accomplished over the years, what you are doing now, so often in the face of enormous challenges, and what you are planning for the future—all of this is evidence of your faith and commitment and the Church is proud of you.

Chapter 13

A Sign of Hope

A Pastoral Letter on Healthcare, October 18, 1995

During my entire ministry as a bishop, especially during the past two years, I have invested considerable time and energy on issues related to Catholic healthcare. When healthcare reform became part of the public policy debate last year, I made several contributions to that discussion—pointing out, for example, the importance of the not-for-profit status of Catholic healthcare institutions. In all of my efforts I have expressed my appreciation for the past and current dedication to, and service in, the ministry of Catholic healthcare by the religious women and men who sponsor this ministry and the dedicated laymen and women who collaborate with them.

Several months ago, I decided to write this pastoral reflection on Catholic healthcare to bring together several of my concerns and to give some direction to healthcare ministry in the Archdiocese of Chicago. However, before I was able to begin the project, I was diagnosed with pancreatic cancer. After surgery at Loyola University Medical Center in Maywood, IL, and a brief period of recuperation, I underwent nearly six weeks of radiation therapy and chemotherapy.

Now I return to this project not only as a bishop with an abiding interest in, and commitment to, Catholic healthcare, but also as a cancer patient who has benefited greatly from this competent, compassionate care in the model of Jesus the healer.

When I entered the Loyola University Medical Center last June, my life had been turned completely upside down by the totally unexpected news that what I had been experiencing as a healthy body was, in fact, housing a dangerous, aggressive cancer. The time since the diagnosis, surgery, and postoperative radiation and chemotherapy has led me into a new dimension of my life-long journey of faith.

I have experienced in a very personal way the chaos that serious illness brings into one's life. I have had to let go of many things that had brought me a sense of security and satisfaction in order to find the healing that only faith in the Lord can bring.

Initially, I felt as though floodwaters were threatening to overwhelm me. For the first time in my life I truly had to look death in the face. In one brief moment, all my personal dreams and pastoral plans for the future had to be put on hold. Everything in my personal life and pastoral ministry had to be re-evaluated from a new perspective. My initial experience was of disorientation, isolation, a feeling of not being "at home" anymore.

Instead of being immobilized by the news of the cancer, however, I began to prepare myself for surgery and postoperative care. I discussed my condition with family and friends. I prayed as I have never prayed before that I would have the courage and grace to face whatever lay ahead. I determined that I would offer whatever suffering I might endure for the Church, particularly the Archdiocese of Chicago. Blessedly, a peace of mind and heart and soul quietly flooded through my entire being, a kind of peace I had never known before. And I came to believe in a new way that the Lord would walk with me through this journey of illness that would take me from a former way of life into a new manner of living.

Nevertheless, during my convalescence I found the nights to be especially long, a time for various fears to surface. I sometimes found myself weeping, something I seldom did before. And I came to realize how much of what consumes our daily life truly is trivial and insignificant. In these dark moments, besides my faith and trust in the Lord, I was constantly bolstered by the awareness that thousands of people were praying for me throughout the archdiocese and, indeed, the world. I have been graced by an outpouring of affection and support that has allowed me to experience ecclesial life as a "community of hope" in a very intimate way.

I have also felt a special solidarity with others facing life-threatening illness. I have talked and prayed with other cancer patients who were waiting in the same room for radiation or chemotherapy. I have been contacted by hundreds of people seeking my advice and prayers on behalf of family or friends suffering a serious illness, often cancer.

This experience of the past four months plays an important role in shaping this pastoral reflection on Catholic healthcare. I have reason to believe that my reflections on my illness as well as on the state and future of Catholic healthcare will help and interest others who are struggling either with illness itself or with the delivery of healthcare services in a rapidly changing social, economic, and political environment.

In this statement I will first reflect on my recent experience of both illness and Catholic healthcare in the light of Scripture. Then I will share some of the key concepts that I have articulated in recent years regarding Catholic healthcare—especially my attempt to define more clearly what is distinctive about Christian healthcare ministry. Finally, I will outline some directions for the future of Catholic healthcare in the archdiocese.

I. A Bishop's Reflection

With people of all faiths throughout every age, Christians value physical and emotional life and health. We value all human life as a gift from God and, therefore, stand as ready stewards to respond to the reality of sickness in the world. We do so as individuals when we expend personal resources to prevent illness and find the best, affordable medical care available when we or someone we love becomes ill. We also do so as a Catholic community when we establish a variety of healthcare services, especially for the poor and most vulnerable in our society. Indeed, Catholics as a group are the largest provider of healthcare under single sponsorship in the United States today. Catholic healthcare continues Jesus' healing ministry and reflects a consistent ethic of life, which requires of us a commitment to preserve, protect, and promote the physical health and well-being of all people.

How do we do this as Catholic Christians? What is the distinctively Christian vocation in caring for those who are ill? What do we need to do when, as Christians, we care for those who are ill?

A Promise of Life in the Midst of Chaos

Let us begin this reflection on the Christian vocation of helping the sick and the suffering by asking, "What is God doing in the world?" We begin to find an answer in the very first chapter of Genesis. The first creation narrative was written at a time of great turmoil in the history of the Hebrew people. The nation had been attacked by the Babylonians; their temple, the center of their life as a community, was destroyed; and many of the people were forced to leave their homes to live in exile. Against this background the narrative speaks of God as doing more than creating life in the world. In fact, in its emphasis that God looked at creation and "saw that it was good, "we are reminded that God gives order, meaning, and purpose to the chaos that at times surrounds or invades our lives.

It should be noted, however, that the biblical narratives do not portray God as conquering and doing away with chaos. Genesis does not describe a cosmic battle in which order triumphs over chaos once and for all. Instead, chaos itself is ordered through God's creative activity. But chaos continues to exist. It is a part of life. At times, it can seem to get the upper hand and overcome the order, purpose, and sense of meaning in our lives. But God's creative work is ongoing. God continues to order the chaos we encounter, making it possible for us to live our lives under his protection.

This is an important lesson for us who live in a world where disease and tragedy can shake the foundations of our faith, of our very being. In its own way, illness is a kind of human exile, a feeling of not being "at home," of being cut off from our former way of life. Depending on the seriousness of the illness and our own resources, we may be separated from our homes, our family or loved ones, our source of income or sustenance. Some are abandoned in their illness by those who are unable or unwilling to care for them. At times, family and friends feel abandoned by the sick person on whom they had depended, or by others who do not share the care of the sick person.

Catholic healthcare continues Jesus' healing ministry and reflects a consistent ethic of life.

People who are ill sometimes speak of being attacked and ravaged by a disease that slowly but inexorably conquers them. They may even speak of their own body betraying them, as they begin to lose control of simple bodily functions, or become weaker, frailer, and more dependent on others. Illness can bring people to question if God has punished or abandoned them. Recently, a13-year-old girl who has cancer asked her parents, "I go to church every Sunday, and many of my classmates don't. Why do I have cancer, and they don't?"

We begin to ask: How can we live with Alzheimer's disease, cancer, heart disease, a disability, or an HIV-related disease? A life of illness or disability may seem to be, for the ones who are ill and/or for those who care for them, virtually impossible to live. And in this desperation some seek a solution in euthanasia or assisted suicide. The question that believers and nonbelievers alike have often faced is: How can I continue to live like this?

None of this is new. Believers through the ages have faced the desperation that sometimes accompanies the chaos of illness and suffering. The many laments in the Book of Psalms give eloquent expression to this pain, panic, and desperation. However, the laments also express a firm belief in the power of God to make it possible for us to live our lives despite the chaos. The first chapter of Genesis lays the foundation for this comforting reminder that God's creative activity includes the promise that we are able to live our lives, even in the face of the chaos of illness and death. God's promise of life is the basis for Christian hope.

Hope and the Christian Life

Why does God make such a promise? Because God loves us. And how do we know of this love? St. Paul tells us that we can see God's love for us in the suffering, death, and resurrection of Jesus. "God proves his love for us in that while we were still sinners Christ died for us" (Rm. 5:8). As the apostle also says, we are called to trust that neither death nor life, angels nor principalities, nothing already in existence and nothing still to come can separate us from that love that comes to us in Christ Jesus (Rm. 8:38-39). This event of God's love, revealed to us in Christ Jesus, is the basis for our hope in the midst of life with all its health and sickness, joy and suffering, birth and death. Trusting in God's love from which we can never be separated, we are confident that it is always possible to continue with life despite the chaos we encounter along our pilgrim journey. This, St. Paul tells us, is our hope (Rm. 8:25).

Let me be clear what I mean by "hope." It is not a hope for something. It is not the expectation that something will happen. Although some people hope for a physical cure, not everyone does. Often people believe that a cure is not possible, or they are too tired to hope to be restored to their former state of health. But, even when a cure is not to be expected, one can still hope. The hope of which I speak is an attitude about life and living in God's loving care. Hope, rooted in our trust of God's love for us in Christ, gives us strength and confidence; it comforts us with the knowledge that, whatever is happening to us, we are loved by God through Christ. So, we need not grieve or despair in the same way as those who do not share in this hope (I Th 4:13-18). Illness need not break us. Even if we remain ill, even if we are to die prematurely, we can still be courageous and confident of God's enduring love for us (2 Cor 5:6-10).

> *Our primary service to those who come to us cannot be for sale.*

Some might think that the primary reason for our hope in time of sickness is the fact that Jesus physically cured in his ministry. It is true that Jesus did cure people of their illness, and it is certainly appropriate for us to hope and pray for cures. However, as Christians, we recognize that Jesus does more than offer a physical cure. More central to his mission is the strengthening of people's faith so that they may live as a people of hope. This is the fuller meaning of Jesus' healing miracles. In the miracle accounts, the central point is not so much that someone is cured, but, rather, that his/her relationship with God is restored and/or deepened through their trust in Jesus' love. It is people's faith in Jesus' love for them that saves them from the despair that can overwhelm people when they encounter chaos in their lives. Jesus helps us see that he is someone we can trust in the midst of chaos, someone through whom we can be filled with hope for the future. If we trust in Jesus' love for us, all life, even a life of sickness or disability, is worthwhile.

Healthcare as a Ministry of Hope

In light of all this, I will now share several basic convictions about the ministry of healthcare.

As Christians, our hope relies on the fact that God's love for us in Christ Jesus is permanent and unchanging. Trusting that we are so loved, we face life, with all its sorrows and joy, with hope. However, it is not enough that we be comforted in our affliction. St. Paul tells us that our own consolation enables us to bring comfort to others in their need:

"Blessed be the God and Father of our Lord Jesus Christ, the Father of mercies and the God of all consolation. He comforts us in all our affliction and thus enables us to comfort those who are in any trouble, with the same consolation we have received from him." (cf. 2 Cor 1:3-4)

As Christians, we are called, indeed empowered, to comfort others in the midst of their suffering by giving them a reason to hope. We are called to help them experience God's enduring love for them. This is what makes Christian healthcare truly distinctive. We are to do for one another what Jesus did: comfort others by inspiring in them hope and confidence in life. As God's ongoing, creative activity in the world and the love of Christ make it possible for us to continue to live despite the chaos of illness, so too our work in the world must also give hope to those for whom we care. Our distinctive vocation in Christian healthcare is not so much to heal better or more efficiently than anyone else; it is to bring comfort to people by giving them an experience that will strengthen their confidence in life. The ultimate goal of our care is to give to those who are ill, through our care, a reason to hope.

Our witness to hope is increasingly important in today's commercialized healthcare environment. There are strong economic pressures to pursue income at the expense of the patient and, in fact, to reduce the patient to a commodity. In this context one of the ways in which we witness to Christian hope is through fidelity to our charitable mission within the healthcare industry. Our primary service to those who come to us cannot be for sale. We can sell pharmaceuticals and surgical services, it is true, but these are secondary. Our distinctiveness cannot be turned into a commodity and sold. The moment we shift our motive to one of profit, we will, in fact, undermine our primary mission. Few will find hope in God's love for them if others make a profit from such care.

More importantly, we must recognize the absolute necessity of being present as a community to others in their need if they are to gain confidence in life. Human life is not meant to be lived in isolation. To be fully human, we must live in community. It is very important that a person who is ill have others with whom to communicate. Those who are ill can experience God's enduring love for them through the loving care and concern of the Christian healthcare community. We also serve as a community of conscience for the rest of healthcare.

We are also to give people an experience of God's enduring love for them through a nonjudgmental approach to illness. We do not make a theological or moral distinction between health and sickness. We do not, as Jesus did not, suggest that illness is a punishment for sin (Jn. 9:2-7). Our nonjudgmental welcome of the person who is ill, like Jesus' nonjudgmental welcome of the Samaritan leper (Lk. 17:11-19), gives people an experience of hope by delivering them from the isolation or abandonment that the sick fear most. A judgmental attitude toward illness and disability cuts people off from community and erodes or even destroys hope. Our hospitality saves people from such isolation. Like Jesus, we strive through our hospitality to give people the strength, comfort, and consolation of hope.

A judgmental attitude toward illness and disability cuts people off from community and erodes or even destroys hope.

We seek to do more than merely cure a physical illness. Like Jesus, we heal the whole person. We care for people in such a way, that, whether or not we can physically cure their illness, they find strength and comfort in knowing God's abiding love for them, despite their experience of chaos.

To illustrate this point more fully, let us reflect briefly on two biblical accounts of illness: that of Job in the Old Testament and that of a paralytic in the Gospel of Mark. The contrast of the roles played by the sick persons' friends in these two accounts gives us a powerful insight into the kind of approach we Christians are called to take toward those who are ill.

You will recall that, as the Book of Job opens, Job is faced with several disasters, including the loss of his livelihood, his children, and his health. As a man of great suffering, he is in need of comfort and hope, but he does not get it from the three friends who come to talk with him. Instead, they accuse him before God, telling him to repudiate the sin that he must have committed. Job, who knows of his innocence, is left alone, abandoned by those who ought to have offered him comfort and hope. At the end of the book, after God has spoken to him, Job acquires hope sufficient enough to continue living, but his suffering, his experience of chaos, remains a deep mystery to him.

The approach of Job's friends stands in stark contrast with that of the friends of the paralytic (Mk 2:1-12). While Jesus is teaching in Capernaum, so many people come to hear him that there is no room for anyone else in the house. Then a paralytic, carried by four friends, arrives. Unable to get in through the door, they climb to the roof, make a hole in it, and lower the paralytic down before Jesus. We know from the context of the story that the paralytic is seeking forgiveness for sin. But unlike Job's friends, the paralytic's friends do not accuse him before Jesus. Far from abandoning him in his illness or suggesting that he was in some way responsible for his plight, these four devote themselves to caring for their friend. They save him from isolation, and their friendship gives him a reason to have hope, even in the midst of his paralysis.

Jesus sees the man lowered before him, but takes particular note of those who lowered him. We are familiar with Jesus' words to other individuals who are ill: "your faith has saved you." In this text, however, we read that Jesus saw the four friends' faith (Mk. 2:5). He commends their faith, not the paralytic's. The four friends believe in God's enduring love for them revealed in Jesus, and they find their hope and comfort in him. It is this deep faith and comfort that enables them to console the paralytic, remaining with him as a reason for him to hope. This is the heart of Christian healthcare: caring for people in such a way that they have hope.

Although illness brings chaos and undermines hope in life, we seek to comfort those who are ill, whether or not they can be physically cured. We do so by being a sign of hope so that others might live and die in hope. In this we find the Christian vocation that makes our healthcare truly distinctive. It is the reason we are present to believers and nonbelievers alike.

II. A Bishop's Ministry

One of the benefits of reflection is that it allows us to see reality in a new, fresh way. Although the object of our reflection stays the same, our understanding is deepened or enhanced. Speaking of the Catholic healthcare ministry as a sign of hope enriches an already fruitful ministry. It also serves as a source of motivation and inspiration, especially when we seem to be "losing control" of the ministry. Likewise, it is a powerful standard against which we continually evaluate all that we do.

As we know, however, the health ministry is situated in an environment that is evolving rapidly as a result of technological change and institutional forces. Today, healthcare delivery is no longer centered in the free-standing, acute care hospital. There are several reasons for this. Increasingly, healthcare is focused not only on curing illness but also on preventing illness and building "wellness." Similarly, healthcare is no longer focused solely on the patient but also attends to the overall health of the community. Further, the provision of healthcare is understood as an integrated process that involves many in the community: physicians, nurses, social workers, therapists, ambulatory care sites, physical therapy and rehabilitation centers, long-term care facilities, hospice programs, home nursing, local parishes, chaplains, pastoral care ministers, and individuals as well as the more traditional, community-based, acute care hospital.

Concurrent with these more "philosophical" changes, healthcare has experienced many external challenges. Over the years changes in the administration of federal entitlements (such as Medicare and Medicaid) and the concerns of those who purchase healthcare insurance have sought to constrain the escalating cost of providing healthcare. These realities precipitated a discussion at the national level about the possibility of systemic reform of the provision and financing of healthcare in the United States.

As followers of the Lord Jesus and as citizens of this nation, the U.S. Catholic bishops participated in that debate and articulated several principles that should guide healthcare reform. I personally participated in the discussion through my address at the National Press Club in Washington, DC, in March 1994, where I highlighted several key concepts. The points I made then remain relevant today, even though the context has changed somewhat. (See **Appendix A**.)

The same forces, and others, that precipitated the national debate unfortunately were insufficient to overcome the resistance that emerged from many sources. Although the systemic reform that I and many others advocated has not been realized, the debate did require us as a Catholic community to step back and reflect on why and how we continue the Lord's healing ministry as a sign of hope. Assisted by the many significant contributions of the Catholic Health Association (CHA), as well as by the efforts of the many religious congregations that sponsor Catholic healthcare and countless individuals in the ministry, we have renewed our dedication to Catholic healthcare. I certainly have done so.

In the context of these national and ecclesial movements I developed a Protocol to inform and guide the making of important decisions by Catholic healthcare institutions in the Archdiocese of Chicago. Central to that Protocol (issued in August 1994) is my belief that healthcare is a ministry of the entire community of faith, the Church. Indeed, it is an essential ministry. Therefore, each healthcare institution or system should see itself as part of the whole Church, sensitive to the needs of Catholic healthcare and the other institutions within the archdiocese. So, it is very important that we have both a vision and the strategies necessary to ensure that this essential ministry:

Is available throughout the archdiocese and especially to the poor and marginalized, women and children, the aged and the disabled

Adapts to changing conditions so that it can provide quality and cost-efficient care

Is carried on in a such manner that the decisions of the individual Catholic healthcare institutions contribute to the well-being of the entire ministry and not bring undue harm to other Catholic institutions

Is faithful to our beliefs and values when entering into relations with other than Catholic organizations.

The last point is included because, in the future, healthcare will increasingly be provided in the context of what is often described as "integrated delivery." As a result, Catholic healthcare will find it necessary to enter into relationships with organizations, systems, and businesses that may share some but not all of our values. Of itself this is not bad. The Second Vatican Council taught us about the goodness that can be found in secular culture as well as about our responsibility to be present to culture and society as a leaven of transformation. In fact our mutual collaboration with other people of good will could help us bring about national healthcare reform.

However, as we seek to realize the above goals, two obstacles stand in our way. One is internal, and the other is external.

Catholic healthcare will find it necessary to enter into relationships with organizations, systems, and businesses that may share some but not all of our values.

Let me begin with the internal. The strength of Catholic health ministry has been grounded in the charisms of the many religious communities that have carried on the Lord's healing ministry. In a way, diversity of background, heritage, and religious sensitivities were the energizing forces that made possible the establishment of Catholic healthcare ministry across this nation in response to unique needs, whether they were ethnic, geographic, or other. Today, however, that historical diversity at times seems to get in the way of the future.

What do I mean? The various forces that are propelling change in what is often called the healthcare "industry" are requiring greater collaboration, as I noted earlier. From a strictly business perspective it would seem obvious that those healthcare institutions which share a common value and vision would want to enter such increased collaboration from a position of strength. They would want to ensure:

1. That there would always be "space" for their religiously based "product" in the "evolving market," and

2. That, insofar as possible, they would have the ability to influence the community and others in a positive manner.

And it would seem this would also be the desire of institutions whose "product" is the healing comfort and hope of Jesus.

Often, however, this does not seem to have been the case. The diversity of the past seems to be an impediment to developing the type of collaboration on a local, regional, or national level that will allow us to adapt, as needed, to current trends in order to ensure our ongoing presence as well as our ability to influence the national culture of healthcare delivery. Indeed, at times it has been easier for religious-sponsored institutions to join with nondenominational entities than with other Catholic institutions.

As a bishop, I have responded to this obstacle in several ways. On the local level, I have been committed to the development of a network of Catholic healthcare institutions that will meet the goals and objectives I have mentioned. At the national level, I have encouraged my brother bishops and Catholic healthcare leaders to take the steps necessary to prepare for the future. It would be a tragedy if we did not have the courage to move beyond the past and have the creativity to address the future. I hope that:

> Religious congregations will continue to deepen their trust of one another as they ask themselves how they can ensure the future of the entire ministry as well as the future of their own respective institutions;
>
> Local boards, medical staffs, administration, and employees will enhance appropriate institutional or financial self-interest with a more "Catholic" perspective responsive to local, regional, and national health ministry;
>
> Diocesan bishops will experience "collegiality" in a new way as integration and consolidation challenge the divisions or isolation sometimes caused by diocesan boundaries.

Now to the second, external obstacle. We are experiencing a troubling trend in our nation: viewing healthcare primarily as a business commodity. The most evident manifestation of this is the movement to transform healthcare delivery from a not-for-profit to an investor-owned status. I reflected on these concerns in an address to The Harvard Business School Club of Chicago on January 12, 1995. (See **Appendix B**.) In quite strong terms I urged that all involved in the Catholic health ministry join with others to ensure the continued viability of not-for-profit healthcare in our nation.

The primary focus of that address, however, was on the status of healthcare delivery, whether it be sectarian or nonsectarian in nature. While I remain convinced that the reasons outlined in that address apply in a special way to Catholic healthcare, serious questions have recently been raised within the Catholic community about the compatibility of the Catholic healthcare ministry and investor-owned enterprises.

Because of these questions and other forces, we must carefully identify again that which makes the Catholic healthcare ministry truly distinctive and which organizational structures best preserve and nurture that distinctiveness. As a person of faith, I believe this time of challenge is a "happy fault" that will give us the opportunity to understand better the healthcare ministry as a sign of hope. As the Jewish theologian, David Hartman, reminded our group during my recent pilgrimage to Israel, when we confront another who is different from ourselves, we can better discover our particularity, our distinctiveness.

Overcoming these obstacles will not be easy. While confronting the demands of the changing reality of healthcare, we continually will have to ask ourselves two questions:

1. Can we make a successful transition to the new way of doing the "business" of healthcare?

2. Does this new way lend itself to our Catholic mission and values, especially our being a sign of hope? Most secular providers, including the not-for-profits, have to address only the first question.

As we strive to answer these general questions, we Catholics will also face some more specific questions:

> As the focus of healthcare moves from acute care to the organized practice of medicine within integrated delivery networks, how can we become "sponsors" of this form of healthcare?
>
> How can we sponsor HMOs, or own vehicles for providing insurance or other forms of securing adequate access to healthcare services?
>
> Can we ever sponsor investor-owned organizations?

> Can we work closely with or engage in joint ventures with investor-owned organizations or organizations whose mission and value base are possibly not compatible with our religiously based tradition?

In light of my earlier reflection, I suggest that, as we work to answer these questions, we do so keeping in mind that our ministry is distinctive because it is a sign of hope.

In what follows I cannot address all of these issues. They will have to be answered collaboratively by all who are involved in healthcare ministry. To that end I am encouraged that Catholic healthcare leaders are coming together at this crossroads for healthcare and fully support the "New Covenant" initiative sponsored by the National Coalition on Catholic Health Care Ministry, the Catholic Health Association, and Consolidated Catholic Health Care.

III. A Bishop's Proposals

In anticipation of that process I now will offer some pastoral guidance on several matters pertaining to the Catholic healthcare ministry. I will speak as a bishop who, with his brother bishops, is responsible for addressing moral and ethical issues that confront us as a nation as well as for engaging those pastoral concerns that are common to the life of the Church in the United States. In this larger context I will also speak as pastor of this local church about the healthcare ministry in the Archdiocese of Chicago.

Social Issues

I was deeply disappointed by our inability as a nation to move forward with systemic reform of our nation's delivery of healthcare. While now is not the time to attribute blame, I am troubled that our constitutional process for decision making seems increasingly incapable of addressing fundamental issues. We have become a nation of "sound bites" and "special interests." More recently, we have also become ever more comfortable with an "ethic of punishment," which seeks to replace an ethic of personal and social responsibility.

As persons of faith, we believe that these trends require that we become more and more involved as voices of conscience within the political process. In a very special way we must become more adept at challenging the "what-am-I-going-to-get-out-of-this" mentality. We can do this by sharing some Catholic insights. First, we must share with others our Catholic vision of the human person as someone who is ultimately grounded in community. The vision of human solidarity of which I spoke earlier is the best antidote to a sense of alienation and isolation that ironically often expresses itself in an exaggerated attention to personal needs and desires.

Second, while encouraging the movement toward a greater sense of personal accountability and personal responsibility, we must share with others our convictions about the need for compassion, the existence of the common good, and the responsibility of society and government to promote the common good. An unbalanced attention to personal responsibility can become the excuse for neglecting our social responsibilities. While we can never condone or endorse personal irresponsibility, such irresponsibility does not destroy a person's innate dignity or our social obligations to ensure that all citizens are able to realize their basic human rights.

Our Catholic tradition tells us that those who are poor or marginalized have the first claim on us, as individuals and as a society.

A third Catholic insight—one that is more difficult for some to accept—is our responsibility toward the poor. Our Catholic tradition tells us that those who are poor or marginalized have the first claim on us, as individuals and as a society. While this expectation is grounded in a deep faith conviction, it also flows from a Catholic understanding of social justice. This philosophy of society says that the state has two responsibilities. Many agree with the first, that government should do nothing to impede or violate fundamental human rights. In regard to the second responsibility, that government is to create those conditions necessary to realize those rights, people of goodwill may disagree on how to define such rights and are even more likely to argue over how one describes those conditions. Such a debate and discussion are healthy for a nation.

However, it seems to me that today the real debate, especially in the current discussion about welfare reform, is about whether to affirm or deny the second responsibility. In fact, in certain quarters I sense a mean-spiritedness that, under the guise of encouraging responsible living, is, in fact, judging the poor and the marginalized as a class or social group who are responsible for their situation. The logical conclusion of this judgment is that society need do nothing. And because we are now in the realm of so-called "personal failure," some have concluded that the not-for-profit sector of society, and in particular religious institutions, and not the government, should care for the needs of such people. After all, it is argued, it is religion that helps people to achieve a moral conversion.

In addition, while it is true that much of what presently exists as welfare programs can and should be improved, our efforts at reform cannot ignore the reasons why current programs or entitlements were created in the first place. Over the last half-century, we have come to recognize certain human and social needs, which, as a nation, we could not ignore. In effect, we concluded that in these areas the demands of the common good required action. Attempts to eliminate inefficiency and ineffectiveness must be carefully evaluated to ensure that, intentionally or unintentionally, they do not result in our walking away from these communal and social responsibilities.

Obviously, we must do all in our power to ensure a proper ethical foundation for public policy in this and other aspects of our common life.

I make note of all this in a pastoral reflection on the ministry of healthcare for two reasons. First, the decisions the federal and state governments make on welfare reform will have an immense impact on the provision of Catholic healthcare. Because we consider the provision of healthcare as a social good, we are present where others will not go. That presence, however, has been assisted in recent years by state and federal entitlements. If that assistance is eliminated or significantly reduced, many people, especially the vulnerable, will not be served. In particular, many of our "disproportionate share" hospitals (those that serve a large number of patients who have no insurance or personal means of paying for healthcare) will find it extremely difficult to continue. While we will do all we can to preclude such closings, the suggestion that religious organizations should be able to replace government dollars with charitable dollars is, at best, naive. It is not realistic to assume that parishes, churches, and synagogues will be able to offset through their charitable activity the withdrawal of government support.

How can we revitalize the "Catholic imagination" of healthcare that sustained and challenged those who went before us?

Second, if such regrettable decisions are made, we will have to find new ways of meeting the healthcare needs of those who are being abandoned by society. The poor, who will come to us because of a governmental retreat, must become the occasion for a new creativity on our part. While our presence will be different, we must still be there for those in need. How we achieve such solidarity will require the involvement of the entire community of faith.

Catholic Healthcare

I now would like to address my sisters and brothers who exercise positions of leadership in the healthcare ministry. We are at a turning point, at a critically important moment. While some have concluded that this is "the beginning of the end" of Catholic healthcare as we have known it, it can be a time of "refounding." Previously I noted some of the changes that would help this "refounding" to occur: developing greater trust and more effective collaboration among religious congregations, moving beyond institutional self-interest that excludes the common good of Catholic healthcare, and entering into a new sense of episcopal collegiality.

These seem so self-evident that one immediately begins to wonder why it appears so difficult for them to be realized. I offer one possible explanation for this difficulty: Catholic healthcare has become more of a business than a ministry. As healthcare has become increasingly expensive, quite complex, and ever more sophisticated, we necessarily have had to become more focused on economic, technological, systemic, and complex medical realities in a predominantly acute care setting. Could it be that, despite our best intentions and efforts, these forces may distract us from an interiorization of the vision of healthcare as a sign of hope? To say it another way, how can we revitalize the "Catholic imagination" of healthcare that sustained and challenged those who went before us? Unless we attend to this spiritual and formational vision, we will not be able to experience the rebirth we all desire. Economic, technological, systemic, and medical realities are not enemies. Rather, it is also to them that we bring our ministry of Christian hope.

The Archdiocese

Now I will address the Church in Cook and Lake counties, IL, and indicate some directions we need to pursue as a local church. In order to realize them, we must work together as one family of faith.

First, I challenge the parishes of the archdiocese to become more vigorously engaged in forming people and communities of hope. As Jesus himself lived and taught, it is in the midst of the Christian community that God's word of hope is proclaimed and people of hope are formed and nourished. The parish is a vital place for education and formation, for bringing the resources of our faith to bear on how we interpret and respond to the experiences of aging, illness, and dying in the local community. Historically, the parish community has responded to the spiritual needs of its sick and elderly. The parish needs to reclaim its sacred responsibility by calling forth and training leaders and groups to provide a powerful witness of God's care for those suffering sickness or struggling with the process of aging. Our unique vocation in healthcare will not be fully achieved unless it is rooted first in our parish communities, and our parish communities, in turn, collaborate more effectively with other ecclesial institutions, such as Catholic Charities.

Second, I encourage Catholics to take advantage of Catholic healthcare. In saying this, I realize that often the first decision people make is about which physician they will consider "their doctor." They then go to the hospital at which their doctor serves or one that is most convenient geographically. For others, the choice is more restrictive, depending on the type of healthcare coverage or plan that is offered by their employer. Nevertheless, I encourage individuals and employers to consider and support Catholic healthcare systems and institutions. I say this not out of an outdated sectarianism but because of a profound belief that Catholic healthcare can and should provide an environment of faith-filled hope in face of the chaos that accompanies serious illness. Catholic healthcare envisions working in partnership with parishes and others to develop healthy communities. And a vibrant Catholic healthcare will have the resources necessary to carry on our ministry to those in need. I strongly encourage pastoral leaders in our parishes and agencies to add their own encouragement.

Third, we must ensure that the vision of the Catholic healthcare ministry outlined in my meditation is truly present in our Catholic healthcare institutions. To achieve this end, I ask the Catholic Health Alliance of Metropolitan Chicago (CHAMC) to develop a joint committee representing sponsors and management as well as representatives of the archdiocese. The task of this committee, using work already done by the Catholic Health Association and others, will be to propose ways to identify and implement standards for evaluating the Catholic character of our healthcare institutions and programs. I do not envision these standards as punitive. Rather they will raise up the best of who we already are in order to ensure that what we proclaim is what we provide. They will complement the necessary movement within Catholic healthcare to ensure the existence of high-quality, cost-effective, community-based services by guaranteeing that our services are also value-based.

Fourth, because the leadership of our Catholic healthcare institutions is more and more the responsibility of dedicated laypersons, we need to ensure the ongoing theological and spiritual formation of all levels of healthcare leadership in the archdiocese. While primary responsibility for such formation belongs to the particular institution, we need to explore how we can ensure that this is done effectively. I therefore ask that

CHAMC, in conjunction with the Center for Development in Ministry, research what is currently available, including CHA resources, and how this formation can be enhanced.

Fifth, I have a direct responsibility for overseeing the pastoral or spiritual care of patients in Catholic healthcare institutions. I know that our healthcare facilities are committed to providing this important service and that they see it as essential to their identity. I am asking that the Archdiocesan Office for Health Affairs bring together representatives of pastoral care departments in our facilities, along with skilled pastoral practitioners whom I will appoint, to review the issues confronting the provision of effective spiritual care and to make appropriate recommendations for its ongoing transformation. Such care must attend to the manner in which physical, emotional, and spiritual needs intersect in a person whose life is lived in the environment of family and friends, as well as business, social, and other relationships. Consequently, this spiritual care, while respecting the conscience and privacy of those it serves, must be better integrated with parish pastoral services. In this way it can become an effective catalyst for healthcare being a ministry of hope to all it touches.

Sixth, I again express my support for the creation of an effective archdiocesan Catholic healthcare network. While such a network is but a first step in what I hope will be a process of increased collaboration, it is a very important step. I commend those who have already decided to participate. Unfortunately, at this time, not all of our Catholic acute care institutions have decided to participate in the network. I will continue my discussions with those institutions with three goals in mind: achieving effective collaboration within the Catholic ministry; avoiding actions that will bring unjustified harm to others who share in the Catholic ministry; and preserving Catholic integrity and identity.

Seventh, because our healthcare ministry continues Jesus' healing work, the archdiocese will initiate discussions with other institutions and systems in the Chicagoland area that also carry on the Christian mission of healthcare. Our commitment to developing effective avenues of ecumenical cooperation, as well as the common needs we share as faith-based organizations, requires such dialogue. This is particularly true of the Episcopal and Lutheran communities with whom we have entered into covenantal relationships.

Eighth, we must review our own archdiocesan and parochial ministries to those who experience permanent or transitory healthcare challenges, in particular, those who experience mental or emotional illness.

Often these persons and those who care and support them have not felt the support and encouragement of their brothers and sisters in faith. I ask that the Office of Health Affairs review these efforts and make appropriate recommendations for consideration by the Archdiocesan Pastoral Council and Presbyteral Council. This review also should pay attention to the manner in which we provide for the spiritual and sacramental needs of those who are homebound or in other than Catholic institutions.

Finally, I ask that all those who share in the responsibility for carrying on Jesus' healing ministry join me in resisting efforts to make healthcare in our nation or our own ministry merely another commodity, simply another item to be sold.

Personal Thoughts

Now, I will close with some personal thoughts.

As I said at the beginning of this pastoral reflection, I have recently experienced personally the chaos that accompanies illness. I have had to let go of some things that I thought brought me security in order to find the healing that only faith in the Lord can bring. I have been graced by an outpouring of affection and support that has allowed me to experience the Church as a community of solidarity and a sign of hope in a very intimate manner. I am grateful for this because it has strengthened my confidence, my hope that in Christ life can be lived, even with pancreatic cancer.

In the context of this new moment in my own pilgrimage I offer this pastoral reflection to the Church. May it be for all who encounter it an opportunity for personal reflection and rededication. May we always be a people "who comfort those who are in any need with the same consolation we have received" (2 Cor. 1:4) from the Lord.

Appendix A

Key Concepts of Address to National Press Club (March 1994)

1. In this current debate, a consistent ethic of life requires us to stand up for both the unserved and the unborn; to insist on the inclusion of real universal coverage and the exclusion of abortion coverage; to support efforts to restrain rising health costs; and to oppose the denial of, or retrenchment in, providing needed care to the poor and vulnerable.

2. We have been drawn into a discussion of fundamental values and social convictions. And these convictions find their origin in a vision of the human person as someone who is grounded in community, and in an understanding of society and government as being largely responsible for the realization of the common good.

3. Healthcare is an essential safeguard of human life and dignity, and there is an obligation for society to ensure that every person be able to realize this right.

4. The only way this obligation can be effectively met by society is for our nation to make universal healthcare coverage a reality. Universal access is not enough.

5. Universal coverage is not a vague promise or a rhetorical preamble to legislation, but requires practical means and sufficient investment to permit everyone to obtain decent healthcare on a regular basis.

6. If justice is a hallmark of our national community, then we must fulfill our obligations in justice to the poor and the unserved first and not last.

7. If real reform is to be achieved—that is, reform that will ensure quality and cost-effective care—then we must do what is necessary in order to ensure that our healthcare delivery system is person centered and has a community focus.

8. Our objective must be a healthy nation in which the mental and physical health of the individual is addressed through collaborative efforts at the local level. The poor, vulnerable, and uninsured persons cannot be denied needed care because the health system refuses to eliminate waste, duplication, and bureaucratic costs.

9. In light of these concerns, the nation must undertake a broad-based and inclusive consideration of how we will choose to allocate and share our healthcare dollars. We are stewards, not sole owners, of all our resources, human and material; thus, goods and services must be shared.

10. The U.S. Catholic bishops continue to insist that it would be a grave moral tragedy, a serious policy mistake, and a major political error to link healthcare reform to abortion.

11. Fundamentally, healthcare reform is a moral challenge—finding the values and vision to reshape a major part of national life to better protect the life and dignity of all.

Appendix B

Key Concepts* of Address to The Harvard Business School Club of Chicago (January 1995)

1. The healthcare delivery system is rapidly commercializing itself, and, in the process, is abandoning core values that should always be at the heart of healthcare delivery.

2. Healthcare by its nature is not a mere commodity. It is fundamentally different from most goods and services.

3. The primary goals of medical care are wellness, a cured patient, and a healthier community—not to earn a profit or a return on capital for shareholders.

4. A not-for-profit structure is better aligned with these "noneconomic" ends and is more compatible with the essential purpose of healthcare.

5. There are four essential characteristics of healthcare delivery that are especially compatible with the not-for-profit structure but less likely to occur when healthcare decision making is driven predominantly by the need to produce a return-on-equity for shareholders: access to care for costly and hard-to-serve populations; medicine's patient-first ethic; attention to community-wide needs; and volunteerism.

6. Each of us and our communities have much to lose if we allow unstructured market forces to continue to erode the necessary and valuable presence of not-for-profit healthcare organizations here in Chicago and throughout the nation.

* Excerpted from *Making the Case for Not-For-Profit Healthcare.*

CHAPTER 14

Renewing the Covenant with Patients and Society

American Medical Association,
Washington, DC, December 5, 1995

Thank you for your warm welcome and your invitation to speak with you this afternoon. These are turbulent times for medicine and healthcare, especially for physicians, and Dr. James Todd [AMA executive vice president], and Dr. Lonnie Bristow [AMA president], may have felt that, as a pastor, I could give some comfort to you who daily navigate these powerful currents of change. I am really not sure how much comfort I can offer, but I can offer some observations that may help guide your own conduct and that of the medical profession as the pace of change accelerates in the coming years.

Such an offer may sound presumptuous, coming as it does from a priest rather than a physician. So, before going further, let me share some of the experience that led me to this seemingly brash venture.

My many pastoral roles often intersect with doctors, institutions of healthcare, and healthcare policy. I am responsible, for example, for the spiritual care of the sick of the Archdiocese of Chicago of nearly two and a half million Catholics. Within the diocese there are more than 100 healthcare agencies, including 20 hospitals and 28 nursing homes. As a member of the Administrative Committee of the National Conference of Catholic Bishops, I have helped to articulate the conference's views on national health policy and other social issues. I am also a member of the Board of the Catholic Health Association of the United States, which represents about 900 Catholic healthcare providers nationwide.

In these roles I have the opportunity to converse and consult with some of the best minds in medicine and healthcare administration. And I have had the chance to write and speak frequently on the nature of healthcare and its significance in human life, with a particular focus on the importance of not-for-profit institutions. In all of this I have seen access to healthcare as a fundamental human right and discussed the ethical dimensions of healthcare within the framework of the "Consistent Ethic of Life," which I have articulated and developed over the past 12 years.

I also stand before you as someone who was recently diagnosed and treated for pancreatic cancer. I am the beneficiary of the best care your profession has to offer. This experience has shaped and deepened my reflections on the challenges you face as individuals and as a profession.

Your profession and mine have much in common—namely, the universal human need for healing and wholeness. What special qualities do ministry and medicine share?

First, we both are engaged in something more than a profession. Ours is truly a vocation. In its truest sense, it means a life to which we are called. In my own case I was called to both professions. As an undergraduate, I had decided to become a doctor and followed a pre-med curriculum. But long before I graduated, I heard a stronger call to the priesthood.

Second, we both are centered on promoting and restoring wholeness of life. The key words in our professions—health, healing, holy, and whole—share common roots in Old English.

Third, and most fundamentally, we both are engaged in a moral enterprise. We both respond to those who are in need, those who ask us for help, those who expose to us their vulnerabilities, and who place their trust in us.

As someone who has cared for others and who has been cared for by you and your colleagues, I hope you will allow me to speak frankly about the moral crisis that I believe currently grips the medical profession generally and physicians individually.

In speaking of a "moral crisis" I realize that I am assuming a position with which some within your profession would disagree. They would assert that the marketplace is the only valid reference point for evaluating medical practice. I respectfully, though forcefully, disagree with such an assertion. I believe that medicine, like other professions—such as teaching, law, and ministry—does have a moral center, even though this center is under attack. And I think you believe deep down as I do that such a moral center exists and that it must not be lost. Dr. Bristow's priority on medical standards as a hallmark of his administration reflects this concern.

What do I mean when I speak of a "moral crisis" in medicine? I mean that more and more members of the community of medicine no longer agree on the universal moral principles of medicine or on the appropriate means to realize those principles. Conscientious practitioners are often perplexed as to how they should act when they are caught up in a web of economics, politics, business practice, and social responsibility. The result is that the practice of medicine no longer has the surety of an accurate compass to guide it through these challenging and difficult times. In other words, medicine, along with other professions, including my own, is in need of a moral renewal.

My purpose today is not to dictate the details of medicine's moral renewal. Rather, it is to invite you to join me in a conversation that will lead to a restoration of medicine's first principles. I am convinced that, with good will and persistence, this process will benefit society, reinvigorate the medical profession, preserve its independence, and infuse your lives with a quality of meaning that has often been missing.

How did we arrive at this situation? Medicine, like other professions, does not exist in a vacuum. The upheavals in our society, especially those of the past 30 years, have left their imprint on the practice and organization of medicine. Each of us has his or her own list of such upheavals. My list includes the shift from family and community to the individual as the primary unit of society, an overemphasis on individual self-interest to the neglect of the common good, the loss of a sense of personal responsibility and the unseemly flight to the refuge of "victimhood," the loss of confidence in established institutions, the decline in religious faith, the commercialization of our national existence, and the growing reliance on the legal system to redress personal conflicts.

In addition to societal changes, there are causes specific to the medical enterprise that contribute to medicine's disconnection from its underlying moral foundation. For example, advances in medical science and technology have improved the prospect of cure but have de-emphasized medicine's traditional caring function. Other contributors include the commercialization of medical practice, the growing preoccupation of some physicians with monetary concerns, and the loss of a sense of humility and humanity by certain practitioners.

None of this, I am sure, is news to you. In surveys, newspaper articles, and personal conversations, many physicians report that they are increasingly concerned with the condition and direction of medical practice.

Medicine, along with other professions, including my own, is in need of a moral renewal.

What may surprise you, however, is my contention that, to reverse these trends, you, as individuals and as a profession, must accept a major share of the responsibility for where you are today. Physicians have too often succumbed to the siren songs of scientific triumph, financial success, and political power. In the process medicine has grown increasingly mechanistic, commercial, and soulless. The age-old covenants between doctors and patients, between the profession and society, have been ignored or violated.

But I hasten to add this dire view is tempered by hope. If the present predicament is the product of choices—explicit and implicit—made by members of your profession, then it is possible that you can choose to change it.

The change I have in mind is "renewing the covenant with patients and society," that indeed is the title of this presentation. That covenant is grounded in the moral obligations that arise from the nature of the doctor-patient relationship. They are moral obligations—as opposed to legal or contractual obligations—because they are based on fundamental human concepts of right and wrong. While, as I noted earlier, it is not currently fashionable to think of medicine in terms of morality, morality is, in fact, the core of the doctor-patient relationship and the foundation of the medical profession. Why do I insist on a moral model as opposed to the economic and contractual models now in vogue?

Allow me to describe four key concepts of medicine that give it a moral status and establish a covenantal relationship:

- First, the reliance of the patient on the doctor. Illness compels a patient to place his or her fate in the hands of a physician. A patient relies, not only on the technical competence of a doctor, but also on his or her moral compass, on the doctor's commitment to put the interests of the patient first.

- Second, the holistic character of medical decisions. A physician is a scientist and a clinician, but, as a doctor, he or she is and must be more. A doctor is and must be a caretaker of the patient's person, integrating medical realities into the whole of the patient's life. A patient looks to his or her doctor as a professional adviser, a guide through some of life's most difficult journeys.

- Third, the social investment in medicine. The power of modern medicine—of each and every doctor—is the result of centuries of science, clinical trials, and public and private investments. Above all, medical science has succeeded because of the faith of people in medicine and in doctors. This faith creates a social debt and is the basis of medicine's call—its vocation—to serve the common good.

As a society, we must not lose our shared commitment to protect our vulnerable members.

- Fourth, the personal commitments of doctors. The relationship with a patient creates an immediate, personal, nontransferable fiduciary responsibility to protect that patient's best interests. Regardless of markets, government programs, or network managers, patients depend on doctors for a personal commitment and for advocacy through an increasingly complex and impersonal system.

This moral center of the doctor-patient relationship is the very essence of being a doctor. It also defines the outlines of the covenant that exists between physicians and their patients, their profession, and their society. The covenant is a promise that the profession makes—a solemn promise—that it is and will remain true to its moral center. In individual terms, the covenant is the basis on which patients trust their doctors. In social terms, the covenant is the grounds for the public's continued respect and reliance on the profession of medicine.

The first dimension of this covenant deals with the physician's responsibilities to his or her patients. They include:

• First, placing the good of the patient over the interests—financial or otherwise—of the physician, insurance company, the hospital, or system of care. This issue is rarely overt; rather, it springs from a growing web of pressures and incentives to substitute someone else's judgment for your own.

• Second, ensuring that the use of advanced medical science and technology does not come at the expense of real caring. A recent study in the *Journal of the American Medical Association* documented a continuing compulsion to spare nothing for the dying patient, without regard for the patient's dignity, comfort, or peace of mind.

• Third, upholding the sanctity and dignity of life from conception to natural death. "The Consistent Ethic of Life," to which I referred earlier, calls on us to honor and respect life at every stage and in all its circumstances. As a society, we must not lose our shared commitment to protect our vulnerable members: the unborn, persons with disabilities, the aged, and the terminally ill. We must not allow the public debates over the right to life of the unborn person and legalized euthanasia to deter us from our commitment.

• Fourth, attending to your own spiritual needs as healers. As a priest or a physician, we can only give from what we have. We must take care to nurture our own personal moral center. This is the sustenance of caring.

The responsibilities I just noted are not new to the practice to medicine. Almost 2,500 years ago, Plato summed up the differences between good and bad medicine in a way that illuminates many of the issues physicians face today in our increasingly bureaucratized medical system [*The Laws*, Book IV]. In his description of bad medicine, which he called "slave medicine," Plato said,

"The physician never gives the slave any account of his problem, nor asks for any. He gives some empiric treatment with an air of knowledge in the brusque fashion of a dictator, and then rushes off to the next ailing slave."

Plato contrasted this bad medicine with the treatment of free men and free women:

"...the physician treats the patient's disease by going into things thoroughly from the beginning in a scientific way and takes the patient and the family into confidence. In this way he learns something from the patient. The physician never gives prescriptions until he has won the patient's support, and when he has done so, he aims to produce complete restoration to health by persuading the patient to participate."

> *Failure to ground the profession in a strong set of moral values risks the loss of public respect and confidence.*

Similar ideas are reflected in the Hippocratic Oath attributed to an ancient Greek physician. This oath is still used at some medical school graduations. Its second section includes a pledge to use only beneficial treatments and procedures and not to harm or hurt a patient. It includes promises not to break confidentiality, not to engage in sexual relations with patients or to dispense deadly drugs. It specifically says: "I will never give a deadly drug to anybody if asked for it, nor will I make a suggestion to this effect."

There are plenty of pressures, some self-imposed and some externally imposed, that make it easy to practice bad medicine, just as there were two and one-half millennia ago. Sustaining your covenants requires a willingness to affirm and incorporate into your lives the ancient virtues of benevolence, compassion, competence, intellectual honesty, humility, and suspension of self-interest—virtues which many of you live quite admirably, I'm sure, and I congratulate you for it.

Let us move now from the covenantal obligations of the individual physician to the responsibilities of the profession. Medicine is a profession that has the freedom to accredit its educational institutions, set standards of practice, and determine who shall practice and who shall not. As such, it is a moral community subject to a set of moral obligations. First among these obligations is the requirement to enlist and train new members of the profession who befit the nature of the profession. Beyond intellectual ability, you must ask whether potential medical students have the potential to live up to the moral responsibilities of a physician, that is, will they be "good" doctors. In addition, those who teach and counsel medical students must be living models of the virtuous physician, living proof that the values we espouse are not romantic abstractions to be discarded when they enter the "real world" of medicine.

President Bristow has lamented the fact that one-fourth of our medical schools have no formal courses in medical ethics. Such courses should, of course, be required in every curriculum. Important as these courses are, however, they are not enough. Indeed, they run the risk of segregating these matters from the core of students' learning experience. If we do not infuse moral and ethical training into every class and practicum, in residencies, and in continuing education, we have not fulfilled our obligation to our students and the profession.

Finally, I would emphasize among medicine's professional obligations the setting and enforcing of the highest standards of behavior and competence. Although those who defraud government and private insurers, those who are incompetent or venal, those who look the other way at colleagues' wrongdoing are undoubtedly a minority, the profession is demeaned by them and must repudiate them. Your own Code of Medical Ethics speaks directly to this point.

Moreover, when physicians engage in sexual misconduct with patients, the "code of silence" that has protected physician and priest alike must be broken. I offer for your consideration what we have done in the Archdiocese of Chicago in matters of clerical sexual misconduct with minors. An independent review board, the majority of whom are not clerics, evaluates all allegations and presents to me recommendations for action. The participation of these dedicated individuals in this process has not diminished the priesthood, but enhanced it.

Failure to ground the profession in a strong set of moral values risks the loss of public respect and confidence, and with that the profession faces the further erosion of its independence. Society's stake in medical care is too great to sustain the present level of professional autonomy if confidence in the profession declines.

Although I am focusing on what I believe needs to be repaired, I do not overlook or take for granted the great and good works performed by physicians every day—the grueling work in hospital emergency rooms, the treatment of AIDS victims, the care for the poor and the homeless, the pro bono work—to name only a few. I truly commend you for the wonderful things you do each day.

Let me summarize my major points so far. First, the practice of medicine is by nature a moral endeavor that takes the form of a covenant. Second, that covenant involves moral obligations to patients, to the profession, and to society. Third, the moral compass that guides physicians in meeting those obligations needs to be fully restored so that the covenant can be renewed. I have discussed the covenantal obligations to patients and the profession and suggested some guideposts. I turn now to the obligations to society.

Physicians and the profession have a covenant with society to be an advocate for the health needs of their communities and the nation. This function is not as immediate or obvious as the others I have discussed, and in some respects its successful exercise depends on fulfilling those obligations that are more intimate to medical practice. The nature of these obligations may also be more controversial, but let me outline the primary elements of the social obligation.

• First, the establishment of healthcare as a basic human right. This right flows from the sanctity of life and is a necessary condition for the preservation of human dignity. Dr. Bristow has indicated that the opportunity for comprehensive reform of our healthcare system is, to use his own words, "at least two administrations from now." I trust that the medical profession will take this prediction as a challenge, not as something that is inevitable.

• Second, the promotion of public health in the widest possible sense. In addition to the traditional public health agenda—clean water, sanitation, infectious diseases—we must include the health implications of inadequate nutrition, housing, and education. In addition, our public health horizons must include the "behavioral epidemics" engulfing our society—drug and alcohol abuse, violence, children raising children.

• Finally, leadership on the question of how best to protect human life and enhance human dignity in a situation of limited health resources. Although this issue is often framed in terms of rationing, I prefer a different word and a different concept: "stewardship." As a profession, you must take the lead in advising policymakers. This is a matter too important to be left to the government and the insurance companies.

If you sense an urgency in my voice today, it is because I believe, with all my heart, we cannot afford to wait to renew the covenant with patients and society until some indefinite time in the future. The future is about to inundate us now. If we do not reset the moral compass before the flood arrives, our opportunity may be washed away. Let me suggest only a few of the overarching issues we are already contending with: the aging of our society and of the industrialized world, the explosion of genetic knowledge and the potential for the manipulation of human life itself, the revolution in information and the attendant privacy issues. Confronting each of these issues will require our moral compass to be crystal clear and firmly set.

It is my hope that today will mark the beginning of a conversation among all of us concerned with the moral framework of healthcare in the United States, but especially among those of you within the medical profession. If current trends continue, the moral authority at the basis of medicine is in danger of being lost, perhaps irrevocably. You are closest to these issues, and, in the end, your choices will determine our course as a nation and community. Recommitting yourselves to medicine's inherent moral center will give you the strength and the grace to renew the covenant and provide the leadership your patients, your profession, and your nation need and expect of you.

Bibliography

Bernardin, Joseph Cardinal, "The Consistent Ethic of Life and Healthcare Reform," *Origins*, vol. 24, June 9, 1994.

Dougherty, Charles J., *Back to Reform*, Oxford University Press, New York, NY (January 1996).

Dougherty, Charles J., "The Costs of Commercial Medicine," *Theoretical Medicine*, vol. 11, pp. 275-286, 1990.

Kass, Leon R., "Professing Ethically: On the Place of Ethics in Defining Medicine," *The Journal of the American Medical Association*, March 11, 1983, vol. 249, no. 10, pp. 1305-1310.

Pellegrino, Edmund D., "The Medical Profession as a Moral Community," *Bulletin of the New York Academy of Medicine*, vol. 66, no. 3, May-June 1990, pp. 2221-232.

Pellegrino, Edmund D., "The Healing Relationship: The Architectonics of Clinical Medicine," Earl E. Shelp (ed.), *The Clinical Encounter*, D. Reidel Publishing Co., Dordrecht, Holland, 1983, pp. 153-172.

Russell, Christine, "Doctors for the 21st Century," *Washington Post*, September 27, 1994, p. Z12.

Siegler, Mark, "The Sign of Hippocrates: The Medical Profession in the 21st Century," presentation at the 21st Pio Manzu International Conference, Rimini, Italy, October 14, 1995.

Siegler, Mark, "Falling Off the Pedestal: What Is Happening to the Traditional Doctor-Patient Relationship?" *Mayo Clin Proc*, May 1993, vol. 68.

The SUPPORT Principal Investigators, "A Controlled Trial to Improve Care for Seriously Ill Hospitalized Patients," *The Journal of the American Medical Association*, November 22/29, 1995, vol. 274, no. 20, pp. 1591-1598.

CHAPTER 15

Managing Managed Care

International Association of Catholic Medical Schools, Loyola University, Chicago, May 13, 1996

It is an honor to be with this distinguished international assembly of medical educators this morning. I trust that those of you who are not from this country will indulge me as I share some reflections on the transformation of the U.S. healthcare system. Although these reflections are couched in the specifics of our experience, many of the issues involved are universal and are the subject of debate in other countries as well.

The next class of Catholic medical school graduates will begin their careers in the coming millennium. We are inclined to think of such chronological watersheds as defining epochal shifts in human behavior and institutions. In the remaining years of the 20th century we are likely to be barraged with predictions and prophecies of what the new century, and the millennium it ushers in, will bring.

In healthcare, however, history has had a head start. The new epoch has not waited for the new millennium; it is already well under way. Among the significant forces for 21st century healthcare that have defined themselves in the past decade are the following: the explosion of genetic information that brings new hope and new ethical challenges seemingly each week; the aging of our society and of the industrialized world; and the revolution in information that expands our horizons and jeopardizes our privacy.

This morning, I will address the phenomenon that will inform the organization and delivery of healthcare in the next century. You do not have to be a futurist or a prophet to know that this is the phenomenon known as *managed care*. In the United States, with more than half of our insured population in some form of managed care, we have already entered the era of managed care. Our challenge for the coming years is in *managing* managed care to ensure that it contributes to the purposes of healthcare for each person, as well as the common good.

I come to this discussion as a pastor, a bishop, a leader of our National Conference of Catholic Bishops, and a member of the Board of Trustees of the Catholic Health Association of the United States. In these capacities I have, with my colleagues, wrestled with the issues raised by managed care and sought to develop responses compatible with our

Published originally in *Origins*, May 30, 1996.

Catholic heritage and healthcare mission. I have pursued this within the context of "The Consistent Ethic of Life" which I have articulated over the past twelve years.

The purpose of the consistent life ethic is to provide a moral framework for analysis and motivation for action on a wide range of human life issues with important ethical dimensions. The foundation for this framework is a deep conviction about the nature of human life, namely, that human life is sacred, which means that all human life has an inalienable dignity that must be protected and respected from conception to death. It is from this vantage point that we consider the nature and value of managed care.

In its relatively brief history, managed care has become many things to many people:

> To some federal policymakers, it is a way to ensure the solvency of the Medicare program and to stretch Medicaid dollars further.
>
> To teaching hospitals and medical schools, it is a danger to broad-based support for medical research and education.
>
> To some patients, it is the loss of choice of a provider; to other patients, it is a greater array of benefits, including preventive services.
>
> To some ethicists, it is a back door rationing scheme; to others, it is a prudent use of scarce social resources.

Managed care appears to be so many different things, in part, because it is a broad term that covers many different healthcare financing and delivery arrangements. In this discussion, I use the term "managed care" to describe an insurance or delivery mechanism that involves one or more of the following elements:

> Limiting the number of providers serving a covered population, either through direct ownership or employment, or through selective contracting or through some combination of these elements
>
> Adherence by providers to utilization management controls
>
> Incentives for patients to use only the providers designated by the managed care plan
>
> Some degree of financial risk for providers, ranging from HMOs that assume full risk for the cost of care to contractual arrangements under which carriers and providers share risk.

The diversity of views on managed care stems in part from the great variety of ways in which the elements of managed care are applied. It is also true, however, that part of the controversy about managed care results from its impact on the healthcare system. Many of the traditional healthcare relationships—between doctors and patients, between insurers and doctors, between hospitals and doctors, between patients and insurers, to name a few—are being dramatically affected by the transition to managed care. In some cases, entirely new entities are being created that replace or restructure existing relationships.

In these times of radical change in the U.S. healthcare system, we should not be surprised that there are many opinions and many public policy issues. Healthcare is intensely personal. Each of us and each of our family members has a direct, personal stake in the cost, availability, and quality of healthcare. In addition, since healthcare in this nation is a more than $1 trillion annual enterprise, the financial stakes for government, insurers, employers, hospitals, physicians, and others are also great, as managed care produces new winners and losers in the marketplace.

We must remember, however, that no system of healthcare is an end in itself. We must examine managed care in terms of the nature of health and purpose of healthcare and how it advances or detracts from those purposes. We may also look at managed care in historical terms: Has it brought improvements over the methods of financing and delivery it is replacing? Are there things of value that are being lost?

Healthcare Values

What are the healthcare principles and values against which managed care should be measured? The goal of healthcare is healing. To heal is to restore wholeness, "to make whole that which is impaired or less than whole." Achieving wholeness requires attention not only to the physical condition of the patient, but also to his or her spiritual and social well-being. Further, healthcare is focused not only on curing illness, but also on preventing it and building "wellness." Healthcare focuses not only on the patient, but also on the overall health of the community. No person can be completely well if his or her community is unhealthy, and a community's health is dependent on that of its members. To fulfill these purposes, a healthcare system must embody the following values:

> **Healthcare must be a service**. Care of those who are ill and dying is an important measure of the moral character of a society. Healthcare is an essential social good, a service to persons in need; it cannot be a mere commodity exchanged for profit, to which access depends on financial resources.

Each person's human dignity must be preserved. Because healthcare is critical to human dignity, all persons have a right to basic, comprehensive healthcare of the highest quality.

The common good must be served. Dignity is realized only in association with others. Healthcare must serve the good of the nation and the community—as well as the individual.

The needs of the poor must have special priority. The wealthy and well must not ignore their obligation to help care for the poor and the sick. The health fate of the poor should be tied to that of the average U.S. citizen.

There must be responsible stewardship of resources. Our resources are not unlimited and must be managed wisely. The healthcare system must use economic discipline to hold health-care spending within realistic limits.

Healthcare should be provided at appropriate levels of organization. It should respect local diversity, preserve pluralism in delivery, protect a range of choice, and preserve the relationship between physician and patient.

In considering managed care and its significance for achieving the purposes and values of healthcare, it is important to recognize the context from which managed care springs. Many of the same forces driving the growth of managed care are also propelling changes in other areas of society. In the private sector, global competition has led companies to seek efficiencies through consolidations, downsizings, and reducing the cost of benefits. In the public sector, continuing federal deficits and resistance to tax increases have led to constraints on government expenditures at all levels for all purposes.

The Traditional System

Healthcare has not been immune from the impact of these forces. Indeed, it is regarded by many as a major contributor to excessive costs and inefficiencies of both the public and private sectors. So, the strengths and weaknesses of the healthcare system that existed before managed care are also part of the context of managed care. Before turning to a consideration of managed care, I will briefly describe the healthcare system that it appears to be on its way to replacing.

In this discussion I shall refer to managed care's predecessor as the "traditional" system, although in many respects that system has become prevalent only in the post-World War II years. In its full blossoming, between 1965 and 1985, the traditional system was characterized by:

> A proliferation of clinically and economically independent healthcare providers, such as doctors and hospitals
>
> Employment-based health insurance for a majority, but by no means all, of the nonaged, nonpoor population
>
> Fee-for-service payment for medical services by the individual, employer, private insurance carrier, or government program
>
> A growing government presence both as an insurer for selected populations and as a founder and supporter of healthcare research and education, and
>
> Healthcare institutions, particularly hospitals, and insurers that were predominantly locally based and not-for-profit.

Looking at the strengths and weaknesses of traditional healthcare in terms of the healthcare values I outlined earlier, we see a mixed picture. For those with adequate insurance or sufficient personal resources, traditional healthcare's strengths include maximizing the choice of providers for patients, and clinical freedom for physicians. Subject to broad categories of insurance coverage and general definitions of medical necessity, a patient and a physician had relatively few limitations on treatment options.

The traditional system's weaknesses include the absence of a right to healthcare for all and the lack of a strong commitment to public health.

The traditional system also was characterized by pluralism in the delivery system and by a commitment to the highest quality medicine through public and private support for research and education. The view of healthcare as a service—as opposed to a commodity—was widespread among physicians and not-for-profit hospitals that provided charity care. Paradoxically, however, the advent of government healthcare programs may have eroded the private sector's commitment to healthcare as a service.

The traditional system's weaknesses include the absence of a right to healthcare for all and the lack of a strong commitment to public health. Although mitigated by community-rated health insurance plans and Medicaid, healthcare for the poor remained haphazard. The traditional system contributed little toward the responsible stewardship of resources.

Indeed, for physicians and other providers, the traditional system offered financial incentives to provide unneeded services and no reason for insured patients not to seek additional care, regardless of its likelihood for success. It may be argued that the relentlessly rising costs of traditional care acted as a brake on expanding healthcare services to the poor and the elderly under existing programs as well as efforts to achieve universal coverage as a matter of right.

Managed Care

Managed care is, in part, a response to the perceived problems of traditional healthcare. We are limited in assessing its strengths and weaknesses relative to our fundamental healthcare values because of its relative newness, its many forms, and its still-evolving nature. A key attraction of managed care is that it offers a vehicle for enhancing the value of stewardship. By emphasizing the efficient use of healthcare resources, managed care appears to have contributed to the recent moderation in healthcare cost increases for employers and governments. By extension, managed care offers the possibility, through containing costs, of broadening access to healthcare through stretching government budgets and encouraging more employers to offer coverage to their employees.

Many types of managed care plans, because they are financially responsible for all the healthcare a person may use, have a strong incentive to provide preventive healthcare and careful management of chronic conditions to avoid costly complications. At the same time, however, these incentives can encourage plans to try to limit their enrollment to healthier populations as a "preventive" technique. A final and important strength of many managed care plans is the promotion of quality by identifying, disseminating, and reinforcing the most effective medical practices to their physicians and other providers.

As I have noted, in some aspects, the features of managed care that promote certain healthcare values may threaten others. Financial incentives to conserve resources can lead to providing too few services even as the traditional system can lead to the provision of too many services. Implicit pressures—such as the linking of physician compensation to cost targets—or explicit practice guidelines can result in limitations on access to needed services. Managed care promotes the consolidation of healthcare services—the grouping of doctors, hospitals, and other providers through employment or contracting into networks. This offers economies of scale that contain costs, but also threaten the continued independence of healthcare institutions that contribute to pluralism in our system. I speak here of Catholic and other religiously affiliated or charitable institutions whose missions are explicitly and intimately bound to the poor and the vulnerable. Also, because managed care typically contributes less support for research and medical education than the traditional system, we must examine the needs of these programs, as well as appropriate funding mechanisms.

As I have expressed on other occasions, there can be little doubt that there are good reasons to change our healthcare system, among them to improve the stewardship of our resources. The rapid growth of managed care, however, has heightened concerns that the economics of healthcare may unduly predominate over other fundamental healthcare values. Economics have always played a role in healthcare, but managed care systems require exceptionally large infusions of capital, primarily to fund the data bases and computer systems needed to monitor care and cut costs, and to fund the creation of networks through the purchase of physician practices. The need for such capital has led an increasing number of not-for-profit hospitals to convert to for-profit status or to enter into joint ventures with for-profit hospital companies. And, while the need to produce a return to stockholders may spur continuous efforts to improve efficiency, it also raises the concern that managed care plans may be tempted to achieve efficiencies by restricting needed care.

RATIONING

Many of the concerns about managed care are related—directly or indirectly—to this fear: namely, that the economic imperatives of managed care will result in the inappropriate rationing of healthcare services. If we accept, as we must, that our resources are finite, then we must address this issue openly and clearly. The very concept of rationing is explosive. I prefer the concept of "stewardship." How do we best protect human life and enhance human dignity in a situation of limited health resources?

If we define rationing as the withholding of potentially beneficial healthcare services because policies and practices establish limits on the resources available for healthcare, rationing becomes an issue of balance between the individual and the community, both of which have acknowledged needs. Under this definition, we do not prejudge the issue of whether a specific proposal or method of rationing is good or evil; we leave open the possibility that withholding care may be justified by limits on resources.

This is not an abstract discussion. Rationing healthcare is a regular, if unacknowledged, feature of both our traditional healthcare system and of our system as modified by managed care. As a nation, we ration healthcare by choosing not to adopt a system of universal healthcare coverage. As a result, nearly 40 million are uninsured and some 50 million more are underinsured. Government programs, such as Medicare and Medicaid, ration access to care on the basis of age, income, and family composition. Private healthcare is rationed by a person's or an employer's ability and willingness to pay. It is also rationed through insurance marketing techniques such as medical underwriting, pre-existing condition exclusion, and redlining.

In my own life, as a person diagnosed with pancreatic cancer, I could have been denied treatment on several different grounds:

> My age—if I had been under 65 (the Medicare qualifying age) and if I had been uninsured
>
> The expected outcome for persons of my age and health, or
>
> Lack of coverage by my health plan for a specific procedure.

I also could have been discouraged, directly or indirectly, from seeking treatment if my physician had incentives to inform me of only certain treatments or incentives to provide needed treatments for my condition in a facility far from my home and loved ones. In my case, however, I was well-insured through a combination of private coverage paid by my diocese and Medicare that allowed me and my physicians maximum flexibility in selecting a treatment regimen.

Rationing healthcare is a regular, if unacknowledged, feature of both our traditional healthcare system and of our system as modified by managed care.

Two years ago, I called for national health reform that assured universal coverage for all Americans, that is, to end the rationing of access to healthcare through denial of insurance. In that context, I pointed out that we would have to undertake a broad-based and inclusive consideration of how to allocate and share our limited healthcare dollars. It is proper, based on a moral consensus, for society to establish limits on what it can reasonably provide in one area of the commonweal so that it can address other legitimate responsibilities. Although the national debate over universal access unfortunately has been stilled for the present, the Catholic Health Association has addressed the ethics of rationing and offered some moral criteria.

These criteria demand that any acceptable rationing plan must: (1) meet a demonstrable need, (2) be oriented to the common good, (3) result from an open and participatory process, (4) apply to all, (5) give priority to disadvantaged persons, (6) be free of wrongful discrimination, and (7) be monitored in its social effects. Although these criteria were conceived in the context of developing a universal health plan, most of them are still as appropriate to the rationing decisions of private health plans as they are to public programs and should be applied to managed care in both sectors.

For example, an employer purchasing a healthcare plan should look not only at price, but also at the policies of any plan that may limit needed care. The employer is obligated to consider whether its resources or those of its employees are so limited as to justify a health plan that relies on rationing. The employer must also be sure that access to any health plan offered is equitable. When employers contribute a greater share of the premium cost for employees earning lower wages, they reduce the potential for rationing based on ability to pay.

Likewise, some states may have a genuine problem raising tax money for their Medicaid programs. But others have simply decided, for political expedience, to maximize, that is, not to diminish some of their citizens' disposable incomes, regardless of the unmet healthcare needs among their poorer citizens. This is irresponsible. Healthcare rationing in this context is unfair.

As I have pointed out, such rationing is not unique to managed care. Indeed, it has been a staple in the traditional system. Under that system, however, rationing although reprehensible, is relatively visible. Managed care may require greater scrutiny to ensure that rationing decisions are transparent to patients and the public.

Managing Managed Care

In terms of the healthcare values we uphold—human dignity, stewardship, the common good—managed care offers both *promise* and *peril.* By restraining costs, it offers the possibility of including more persons under public and private insurance. By explicitly addressing the appropriateness of care through practice guidelines and other means, it offers the possibility of improving the quality of healthcare and eliminating unnecessary care. By focusing on prevention, it offers the possibility of avoiding or mitigating many serious and disabling conditions.

As I have noted, however, the market forces and economic disciplines that are the engines of managed care can be socially insensitive and ethically blind. In managing managed care we must find ways to encourage and sustain its benefits and to constrain those tendencies which, if left unattended, could undermine important healthcare values.

Because managed care is not a single phenomenon, but, rather, a variety of organizations, practices, and techniques that share almost as many differences as commonalities, its deficiencies, present and potential, defy sweeping diagnosis and prescription. At the same time, it is clear that managed care raises issues that go right to the social and ethical core of our healthcare values. As managed care asserts itself as the healthcare paradigm for the next century, we are obligated to confront these issues and shape its development. I have organized my own reflections on managed care around three groupings of issues: (1) those dealing with the *common good*; (2) those affecting the *quality* of healthcare; and (3) issues relating to stewardship and *rationing*.

The paramount healthcare issue of our time is the affront to human dignity that is occasioned by the lack of universal insurance coverage for even basic care.

First, I will address the *common good*, the social dimension of managed care. The paramount healthcare issue of our time is the affront to human dignity that is occasioned by the lack of universal insurance coverage for even basic care. In addition to the fear, insecurity, and inadequate healthcare that afflict individuals, the existence of rural and inner-city hospitals that care for the uninsured is threatened by competitive managed care. While in theory managed care should help free up resources to cover such persons, it is not clear, despite some innovative state experiments, that managed care savings from public programs will be recycled to expand coverage. On the private side, it is a troubling fact that, despite several years of moderation in the growth of employer healthcare costs, which many attribute in large part to the growth of managed care, the number of persons covered by employer insurance has declined, not increased. It is not enough to argue that, without managed care, more persons would lose their insurance. We must use the benefits of managed care to help achieve the broadest possible coverage of our population.

In this regard, we must also develop mechanisms to provide appropriate support for education and research from all participants in the healthcare system. In general, managed care plans avoid sending patients to hospitals and other institutions with primary responsibility for training healthcare professionals and conducting medical research—activities that provide broad public benefits. At the same time, our teaching priorities must be adjusted to produce an appropriate number and balance of specialists and primary care providers. Research must also give greater emphasis to public health issues and behavioral problems.

There remains the potential that economic incentives for doctors and other providers in managed care plans may lead to ad hoc rationing decisions that are designed to protect income, not the patient.

The last social issue I will comment on is not peculiar to managed care, but is one that could be compounded by the competitive environment in which managed care operates. We must develop and adopt methods to compensate health plans that enroll disproportionate numbers of sick people at the expense of plans that enroll disproportionate numbers of healthy people. If we do not, we will witness a morally repugnant system in which plans will compete to avoid caring for the sick, thus avoiding a central purpose of healthcare altogether. These methods, known as "risk adjustment," reduce incentives for managed care plans to compete based on enrolling only healthier populations.

Second, I turn now to a set of issues relating to the *quality* of care. Responsible decisions about managing healthcare depend on good data regarding health outcomes. While increasing attention has been given to this issue by both public and private agencies, much remains to be done. We should take an expanded view of outcomes, going beyond death and illness rates to include functional outcomes, the quality of life from the patient's perspective, and the satisfaction of both patient and provider. Doctors and hospitals should be leaders in the effort to develop and put into use measures of successful care.

These measures should be available to all. Managed care networks should issue annual report cards to the public on their enrollees' demographic characteristics, their health status, the number and kinds of services rendered, and the outcomes of these services. Such report cards will help families choose plans more wisely and will provide the public with the information needed to manage managed care.

Ultimately, quality healthcare is more than the sum of statistical outcomes. The use of practice guidelines should be expanded to include a strong patient role in the decision process. Patient education and empowerment programs have demonstrated better outcomes and lower costs when patients are fully informed and active participants. Most important, the patient's active involvement in medical decisions is a critical ingredient in the preservation of human dignity.

Third, let us consider the issues of *stewardship* and *rationing*. As I mentioned a moment ago, there remains the fundamental challenge of universally assuring access to healthcare. Until this is achieved, some of the rationing implications of managed care pose moral problems. The crux of this problem is that, while universal access creates a floor of benefits, rationing creates a ceiling. We find ourselves moving toward a morally untenable situation in which we are building healthcare ceilings without floors—a regime in which there will be no limits on how little care one might receive, only on how much.

In the absence of universal coverage, however, we must focus on how healthcare ceilings are built. For instance, the adoption of practice protocols and other explicit care-determining policies by managed care plans should include a formal role for physicians participating in the plan, as medical staffs at most hospitals participate in decisions with clinical implications. Plan enrollees should also be consulted and there should be provision for public oversight.

Even with such precautions, there remains the potential that economic incentives for doctors and other providers in managed care plans may lead to *ad hoc* rationing decisions that are designed to protect income, not the patient. Some reward for physicians' efforts to make care more economical is appropriate, but financial incentives to physicians to constrain care should be limited to avoid the potential for less than optimal care. One approach to this problem is contained in recent federal regulations that require Medicare HMOs to limit the financial risk of participating physicians to specified levels. This is intended to reduce possible conflicts between a physician's pocketbook and the patient's needs. In general, financial incentives should cover a group of doctors so that the focus is on promoting efficient practice patterns for all patients, not on rewarding individual physicians for denying care to individual patients.

Information on managed care plans' policies that limit care and physician financial incentives should be made available to all enrollees. Physicians must be free to discuss these issues directly with patients without fear of a penalty. When controversies arise about the appropriateness of care, there must be clear guidelines for appeal within a plan, and physicians should have the explicit role of advocacy on behalf of their patients.

These concerns go to the trust that must be at the heart of the doctor-patient relationship, a trust that in many ways is being challenged today and which we must work to strengthen, as I indicated in a recent address to the American Medical Association (AMA) House of Delegates.

Conclusion

Managing managed care must involve both the public and private sectors, and there are many initiatives toward this end currently under way by individual healthcare systems and others. Large employer and employee coalitions can play an important role by demanding outcomes-based quality measures by plans that seek their business. Healthcare provider organizations, such as the AMA, the National Committee for Quality Assurance, and the Joint Commission on Accreditation of Healthcare Organizations, also have a critical role to play in helping to ensure that managed care contributes to the values of human dignity and social good.

The Catholic Health Association, in its proposal for healthcare reform, entitled *Setting Relationships Right*, has addressed many of these issues. And Catholic health providers, such as Eastern Mercy Health System, Radnor, PA, and Mercy Health System, Cincinnati, OH, have developed explicit ethical guidelines for managed care contract negotiations.

By encouraging prudent use of our resources, managed care can help us achieve broader and, ultimately, universal healthcare coverage. It can help improve quality standards and reduce unnecessary and dangerous medical care. It can promote preventive care and wellness. It can nurture comprehensive primary care relationships between patients and physicians.

Like most human endeavors, however, managed care contains within it the potential for creating as many problems as it solves. Without vigilance and thoughtful, constructive engagement, we could find that instead of expanding coverage, managed care might function primarily as an instrument to ensure that those who now enjoy healthcare coverage continue to do so. This is important—we do not wish to see an erosion of coverage—but it is not enough. We could find that new, unacceptable means of rationing are added to those that already exist. We could find that economic goals supplant health goals. We could find that the trust that is so essential to the doctor-patient relationship might be undermined by financial incentives.

As we approach the new century, changes in the healthcare system will continue to accelerate. By evaluating and responding to those changes in terms of our consistent life ethic and our healthcare values, we have the opportunity and the obligation to manage managed care so that it advances the goals of human dignity and the common good.

Bibliography

Catholic Health Association, *Setting Relationships Right: A Proposal for Systemic Healthcare Reform*, St. Louis, MO, 1993.

Council on Ethical and Judicial Affairs, American Medical Association, "Ethical Issues in Managed Care," *The Journal of the American Medical Association*, January 25, 1995, vol. 273, no. 4, pp. 330-335.

Davis, Karen, Collins, Karen Scott, Schoen, Cathy, Morris, Cynthia, "Choice Matters: Enrollees' Views of Their Health Plans," *Health Affairs*, vol. 14, no. 2, Summer 1995.

Dougherty, Charles J., *Ethical Dimensions of Healthcare Rationing*, Catholic Health Association, St. Louis, MO, 1994.

Gold, Marsha R., Hurley, Robert, Lake, Timothy, Ensor, Todd, Berenson, Robert, "A National Survey of the Arrangements Managed-Care Plans Make with Physicians," *The New England Journal of Medicine*, December 21, 1995, vol. 333, no. 25, pp. 1678-1683.

Kass, Leon R., "Professing Ethically: On the Place of Ethics in Defining Medicine," *The Journal of the American Medical Association*, March 11, 1983, vol. 249, no. 10, pp. 1305-1310.

Kassirer, Jerome P., "Managed Care and the Morality of the Marketplace," *The New England Journal of Medicine*, July 6, 1995, vol. 333, no. 1, pp. 50-52.

Pear, Robert, "Doctors Say HMOs Limit What They Can Tell Their Patients," *The New York Times*, December 21, 1995.

Priester, Reinhard, "A Values Framework for Health System Reform," *Health Affairs*, vol. 11, no. 1, Spring 1992.

Rodwin, Mark A., "Conflicts in Managed Care," *The New England Journal of Medicine*, March 2, 1995, vol. 332, no. 9, pp. 604-607.

Weston, Brent, Lauria, Marie, "Patient Advocacy in the 1990s," *The New England Journal of Medicine*, February 22, 1996, vol. 334, no. 8, pp. 543-544.

Woolhandler, Steffie, Himmelstein, David U., "Extreme Risk - The New Corporate Proposition for Physicians," *The New England Journal of Medicine*, December 21, 1995, vol. 333, no. 25, pp. 1706-1708.

CHAPTER 16

What Makes a Hospital Catholic—A Response

America, May 4, 1996

In the April 16 issue of *America*, Paul R. Torrens, MD, poses a very important question: What makes a hospital Catholic? While the occasion for his posing the question is a situation particular to the Archdiocese of Chicago, his concerns relate to the healthcare ministry of the Catholic Church throughout the United States. I will address the broader themes in these observations. Because I am in dialogue with the religious congregation that sponsors St. Elizabeth Hospital in Chicago, the Poor Handmaids of Jesus Christ, it would be inappropriate for me to comment on the specifics of that case. It is my hope and prayer that this unfortunate situation will be resolved successfully to the satisfaction of all concerned.

Let me begin by sharing with you what I wrote about the Catholic healthcare ministry in my recent pastoral letter, *A Sign of Hope*. Building on the 1981 pastoral letter of the U.S. Catholic bishops, *Health and Health Care*, I proposed that the distinctive vocation of Catholic healthcare "is not so much to heal better or more efficiently than anyone else; it is to bring comfort to people by giving them an experience that will strengthen their confidence in life." Catholic healthcare does this by "being a sign of hope so that others might live and die in hope."

The source of this hope is found in faith. The Catholic healthcare ministry embraces a faith that realizes Jesus' love for us is such that it can save us from the despair that can overwhelm when we encounter chaos in our lives and, in particular, the chaos of illness. "Jesus helps us to see that he is someone we can trust in the midst of chaos, someone through whom we can be filled with hope in the future. If we trust in Jesus' love for us, all life, even a life of sickness and disability, is worthwhile."

That Terrible Sense of Chaos

As a person recovering from cancer surgery, I have personally experienced that terrible sense of chaos. And while it is encouraging to me to know that I am receiving the highest quality healthcare available, it is central to my treatment and recovery that I receive that care within an institution that recognizes me as a human being with spiritual needs, not simply as another opportunity to maximize profits.

While these reflections speak more to the spirituality of our ministry, they are our motivation for carrying on what Pope John Paul II has described as "one of the most vital apostolates of the ecclesial community and one of the most significant services which the Catholic Church offers society in the name of Jesus Christ." They also become one of the essential criteria we use when evaluating contemporary developments in the field of healthcare. Whatever Catholic healthcare does should be done in a manner that allows us to be a "sign of hope."

In this context allow me to speak to some of the points raised by Dr. Torrens.

First, he alluded to a protocol I issued in 1994. Why did I issue this protocol? It is no secret that healthcare in the United States is in a period of profound transformation. In fact, it is reasonable to expect that the pace of such change will escalate in the near future. As a diocesan bishop with responsibility for overseeing and coordinating the ministries within a local church, I wanted to ensure that in the years to come there would be a vibrant, Catholic healthcare ministry in the Archdiocese, though it would undoubtedly be different in form—a ministry that would be present throughout this local church and especially available to the poor and marginalized. The protocol outlines principles to guide future decisions so that this goal can be achieved.

In issuing the protocol, I affirmed the unique and indispensable contribution of women and men religious to the healthcare ministry. They have made the ministry possible. I also recognized and confirmed legitimate spheres of subsidiarity. At the same time I affirmed that the healthcare ministry is not the possession of any one religious community, healthcare institution, or healthcare executive. Rather, it belongs to the entire church.

The Nature of Healthcare Ministry

In the past, this ecclesial perspective has found expression primarily in concern over being faithful to the *Ethical and Religious Directives* with particular attention to life and reproduction issues. More recently, it has been seen that this is too narrow an understanding of Catholic identity. Projects like the Catholic Health Association's "Social Accountability Budget" and the involvement of Catholic healthcare in calling for national healthcare reform have demonstrated a much broader and more nuanced understanding of the nature of Catholic healthcare ministry. These developments are reflected in the recently revised *Ethical and Religious Directives.*

Concomitant with these more philosophical developments, the way of "doing" Catholic healthcare has undergone significant development. Religious communities have formed systems to support their ministry, and more recently we have seen the consolidation of systems into new, more complex entities cosponsored by several religious institutes. The "doing" of the ministry is now a complex, often national enterprise.

I mention all of this because it seems to me that we have not developed ecclesiological categories adequate to the new realities of expanded identity, healthcare as a ministry of the entire Church, and new structures to support the ministry. As Bishop James W. Malone of Youngstown said recently:

> A religious congregation's ministry of healthcare exists within a local church under the overseeing and coordinating ministry of the diocesan bishop. And within that local church it is possible to identify what one might call the "common good" of the healthcare ministry within that Church. Similarly, by way of analogy, there is a "common good" associated with that social aggregate which is a religiously sponsored healthcare system. By what standards or criteria do these two "common goods" relate? Does one have priority over another? How is potential conflict resolved?

Because we have not thought this out together, we do not yet have a good understanding of how we can live with legitimate tensions, let alone how we can resolve them for the good of the Church and the ministry. It is imperative that we enter into the dialogue that is needed to arrive at such an understanding.

But business is not the end of a Catholic healthcare organization; it is the means to achieve its mission.

As we proceed with that dialogue, it is inappropriate to suggest that the pastoral office of the Church, the ministry of diocesan bishop, has no rightful role. Such a perspective would marginalize healthcare as less than essential to the Church's institutional mission. It also betrays a dualism that would distinguish "business" from "mission." How we carry out the business of healthcare speaks to our very integrity. But business is not the end of a Catholic healthcare organization; it is the means to achieve its mission. The executive officer and board of a Catholic healthcare organization must hold themselves—and be held—accountable for how well they harness healthcare's necessary business imperatives to the achievement of its essential mission as Catholic.

The Social Dimension of Healthcare

This leads me to the so-called "for-profit" question. I discussed this complex question in an address to the Harvard Business School Club of Chicago in January 1995. In that address and in the archdiocesan protocol I do not consider the for-profit sector of society to be evil or immoral! Nor do I say that there should be no relationship with for-profit enterprises. In fact, some Catholic healthcare institutions have for-profit subsidiaries. Rather, I ask the question, "Where should healthcare be situated in the United States: in the publicly traded, investor-owned, for-profit sphere or where it has been traditionally situated, in the not-for-profit sphere?" My basic question, in other words, is broader than Catholic healthcare and deals with the social dimension of healthcare itself.

I began the development of my answer to this question with a fundamental premise of Catholic social teaching: that medical care is a fundamental human right and that it is also a social right in the sense that society has a fundamental obligation to provide adequate healthcare, just as it does, for example, to provide elementary and secondary education. At stake then is how we organize and support healthcare in the United States so that these rights can be fulfilled.

Another premise of mine flows from the teaching of Pope John Paul II: There are some "goods which by their very nature are not and cannot be mere commodities." I firmly believe that healthcare is one of those "goods" that are not commodities. Like the family, education, and social services, it is special because it is essential both to human dignity and to the character of our communities. There is then a fundamental difference between the provision of healthcare and the distribution of commodities like automobiles. As I noted in my address to the Harvard Business Club, "The primary end or essential purpose of medical care delivery should be a cured patient, a comforted patient, and a healthier community, not to earn a profit or a return on capital for shareholders." For these and other substantive reasons (with particular attention to our responsibilities as a society toward the poor and marginalized) I have concluded that, as a society, we should resist the movement to move the provision of healthcare into the publicly traded, investor-owned, for-profit sphere of society.

Given this general conclusion, I have grave concerns about Catholic healthcare participating in such a movement. In addition to the social concerns, there is another substantive reason for my concern. Catholic healthcare is an expression of Jesus' healing ministry. As such, it has a sacramental character to it. Consequently, it does not seem inappropriate to ask the question: Can a "sacrament" be something that is bought and sold, in part or in whole, like a commodity? Can a "sacrament" become the instrumentality used to return a profit for an investor-owned company?

I do not think so! As a pastor and as a believer who is also a patient, I do not find our mandate to be a "sign of hope" compatible with the ethos and culture of healthcare as simply an economic commodity. How can a ministry of the Church be bought and sold on the stock market?

Working Together as a Family of Faith

From the mail I have received, it is clear that some consider my position to be simplistic, if not naive. If healthcare is going to survive, it is going to need access to capital. I know this is true. My concern is how and where we find that capital. What amazes me is that many turn first to those who are outside the ministry. Without being parochial or sectarian, I suggest that we begin by working together as a family of faith to address the complex challenges that the business dimension of Catholic healthcare must address in the near future. The fact is that, as an aggregate, the business dimension of Catholic healthcare in the United States is quite strong. Below are some figures that compare the total resources of our ministry with the resources of one of the largest for-profit corporations: Columbia/HCA.

Columbia/HCA	**Catholic Healthcare**
Over 300 hospitals	Over 600 hospitals
60,000 beds	140,000 beds
3 states with 20% share	19 states with 20% share
Revenues $14.6 billion	Revenues over $40 billion
Assets $16 billion	Assets over $44 billion

It is obvious from this comparison that we have a great deal of strength. The problem is that we have not developed strategies or approaches that will allow us to leverage this strength. Our own narrowness or lack of overall vision at times gets in the way of our working together for the future. That is why the "New Covenant Process," sponsored by the major participants in the Catholic healthcare ministry, is such an important venture. I am convinced that, if we work together, we can find both the spiritual and fiscal resources necessary to refound this essential ecclesial ministry in a way that will serve both our Gospel imperatives and our responsibilities to serve the common good.

While it is true that, as we move in this direction, we may have to enter into many different types of relationships with partners who do not necessarily share all of our beliefs and commitments, we should enter them out of a strategic vision, and not because of desperation or self-doubt. All that we do must be done so that, in truth, our ministry will be a "sign of hope." As I said in my pastoral letter, "it would be a tragedy if we did not have the courage to move beyond the past and have the creativity to address the future."